D0062425

THE
ORIGINAL DR. STEVE'S

ALMANAC of CHRISTIAN TRIVIA

A MISCELLANY OF ODDITIES, INSTRUCTIONAL
ANECDOTES, LITTLE-KNOWN FACTS
AND OCCASIONAL FRIVOLITY

FULLY INCOMPLETE, UNALPHABETICAL,
WITH NO CONSIDERATION GIVEN TO CHRONOLOGY

STEVE WILKENS

IVP Books

An imprint of InterVarsity Press
Downers Grove, Illinois

InterVarsity Press
P.O. Box 1400, Downers Grove, IL 60515-1426
World Wide Web: www.ivpress.com
E-mail: email@ivpress.com

InterVarsity Press® is the book-publishing division of InterVarsity Christian Fellowship/USA®, a student movement active on campus at hundreds of universities, colleges and schools of nursing in the United States of America, and a member movement of the International Fellowship of Evangelical Students. For information about local and regional activities, write Public Relations Dept., InterVarsity Christian Fellowship/USA, 6400 Schroeder Rd., P.O. Box 7895, Madison, WI 53707-7895, or visit the IVCF website at <www.intervarsity.org>.

Design: Cindy Kiple
Images: scroll: Jim Larkin/iStockphoto
         banners: iStockphoto

ISBN 978-0-8308-3438-9

Printed in the United States of America ∞

Library of Congress Cataloging-in-Publication Data

Wilkens, Steve, 1955-

 The original Dr. Steve's almanac of Christian trivia: a miscellany
 of oddities, instructional anecdotes, little-known facts, and
 occasional frivolity / Steve Wilkens.
      p. cm.
 ISBN 978-0-8308-3438-9 (pbk.: alk. paper)
 1. Christianity—Miscellanea. I. Title.
 BR121.3.W545 2007
 230—dc22

                                                                                2007011906

| P | 16 | 15 | 14 | 13 | 12 | 11 | 10 | 9 | 8 | 7 | 6 | 5 | 4 | 3 | 2 |
| Y | 20 | 19 | 18 | 17 | 16 | 15 | 14 | 13 | 12 | 11 | 10 | 09 | 08 | 07 |

To Zachary

Who never fails to make me smile

CONTENTS

ACKNOWLEDGMENTS

Thanks to friends who suggested ideas and patiently read through and critiqued portions of the manuscript: Rob, Dave, Gail, Cathleen, Roger, Don, Sheryl, Keith, Blake, Katie and many others.

I am grateful to Blake Firstman and Enzo Cesario for suggesting the almanac format of this book and for Blake's assistance in the shaping the concept.

InterVarsity Press has been a terrific partner in several publishing projects, and Gary Deddo certainly deserves thanks for his editorial direction. I am grateful for their willingness to go way outside the box on this one.

My appreciation goes out to Ray Sorenson for his photographic contribution.

Deb—thank you, thank you, thank you.

WHY NO ONE KNOWS FOR SURE
HOW TO PRONOUNCE GOD'S NAME

The word used most often in the Old Testament for God's name (about six thousand times) is the Hebrew יהוה, transliterated as YHWH (or Yod, He, Waw, He, if you want to get technical about it all). This four-letter name is referred to as the Tetragrammaton, a Greek word that means "four letters." So one of the ironies surrounding this term is why Tetragrammaton, which means "four-letter word," signifies something quite the opposite of what we mean today when we speak of a four-letter word. It also seems a bit ironic that this *Hebrew* word יהוה is designated by a *Greek* word (Tetragrammaton). The biggest irony, however, is why no one is quite sure of the proper pronunciation for such an important and oft-written word in the Old Testament.

In early stages of Israelite religion, this name was in fact regularly spoken. Over time, pronouncing the divine name came to be prohibited out of concern that its use would violate the third commandment, which states that "you shall not take the name of YHWH your God in vain." This then creates the odd situation in which one cannot read aloud the third commandment as written without violating the commandment.

Given this concern about dishonoring the divine Name, in the Judaism of Jesus' day only the high priest would speak the word, and only then on the most holy occasion of the Jewish calendar—the Day of Atonement—when he would enter the holy of holies.

However, when the Second Temple was destroyed in A.D. 70, the priestly structure was also dismantled. Therefore, after a few centuries, no one knew the proper pronunciation of יהוה because no one was allowed to say the Name.

☞ HOW DO YOU SAY YHWH WHEN YOU CAN'T SAY YHWH?

So what does one do when reading Scripture, which contains a word for God in about six thousand places, when you can't say that word? Jewish readers, then as now, would pronounce the word *Adonai*, which means "my Master" or "my Lord," instead of the Tetragrammaton when reading Scripture or praying. In other uses, such as conversation and scholarship, the circumlocution used by many is *Ha-Shem*, or "the Name." Thus, in most translations of the Christian Bible today, the Tetragrammaton is rendered as "the LORD in small caps, although the Jerusalem Bible uses *Yahweh* (see below).

The substitution of *Adonai* for the Tetragrammaton solves a bit of a mystery about the later pronunciation of YHWH in the Christian world. The original Hebrew of Scripture is written in all consonants, and the proper vowel sounds included in the words were remembered as they were repeated through the years. As fewer and fewer Jews spoke Hebrew, a group of scholars known as the Masoretes added marks or points that appear both above and below the consonants. These points helped readers know which vowel sounds should be pronounced in the words.

When YHWH appears in the text, the Masoretes inserted the vowel points for the word *Adonai* to remind readers that they were to say *Adonai* instead of YHWH, a moot point by that time because no one knew for sure how to say it anyway. When you combine the Tetragrammaton with the vowel points for *Adonai*, the word comes out "Jehovah."

"Jehovah," it turns out, then, is a hybrid word containing the consonants of one word יהוה, the vowels of another *(Adonai),* and the influence of Germanic languages that turns the "Y" sound to a "J" and the "W" sound to a "V." It is also almost certainly not the proper pronunciation of the Tetragrammaton, although you will get a spirited argument from any Jehovah's Witness about this (for reasons that should be obvious).

Nevertheless, while there is some degree of certainty about what is *not* the correct pronunciation, the question of the precise articulation of the Tetragrammaton is up in the air. The reason for this, as noted above, is that we are not certain which vowel sounds go where. Many scholars lean toward Yahweh (Yah-way) as the original pronunciation because the Tetragrammaton is quite likely a form of the Hebrew verb "to be." The conversation in which Moses asks God what his name is supports this. God's answer in Exodus 3:14 is, "I AM WHO I AM."

Other options for the vocalization of YHWH also exist. For example, the Elephantine papyri, discovered in Egypt in 1907, suggest that the Tetragrammaton might be sounded as Ye-Hoo or Ya-Hoo, thus raising the odd possibility that one might "Google" the word *Tetragrammaton* and end up at Yahoo!

☞ ONE FINAL IRONY FOR THOSE HOPELESSLY ATTRACTED TO MINUTIAE

English speakers are aware that certain consonants in that language can take on vowel sounds when combined with other letters. This is also the case with Hebrew, and that fact makes the quest for discovering the correct pronunciation of the Tetragrammaton even more complicated. As it turns out, each of the three consonants (one is repeated) in the Tetragrammaton can also be transliterated as vowels rather than consonants. In fact, the first-century Jewish historian Josephus states that the Tetragrammaton consists of four *vowels*, in which case the transliteration would be IAUE rather than YHWH.

Thus, one last irony in our story of the Tetragrammaton is that the four consonants, which we cannot pronounce because we don't know what vowels are to be inserted, may actually be four vowels. Are you as confused as Dr. Steve is?

B.C./A.D.

One subtle reminder of Christianity's influence on our world is the fact that most of the world calculates the years on a calendar keyed to the life of Christ. Thus, years designated by "B.C." (before Christ) refer to years prior to Jesus' birth, while those designated "A.D." (*anno Domini* = "year of our Lord") number years following his birth. An interesting irony, however, is that the method of numbering years by B.C. and A.D. did not begin until A.D. 525. In some sense, then, the year A.D. 1 did not exist until 525 years after it happened.

☞ KEEPING TRACK OF TIME

Christianity was born in the middle of the Roman Empire, both geographically and chronologically. The empire determined its years according to the traditional date of the establishment of Rome. This founding date was labeled 1 AUC (*Ab Urbe Condita* = "from the foundation of Rome"), which would be 753 B.C. by our current system. Such standardization was made necessary by the character of the empire itself, which was formed by conquering and incorporating smaller kingdoms.

Prior to this time, most nations numbered years in reference to the reign of the current king. Thus, for example, twenty years into the reign of King Bubba (as far as we know, history does not contain any actual King Bubbas except for the one at the Arkansas Grits Festival), documents would read something like, "in the twentieth year of King Bubba." You can only imagine the perplexity caused by trying to maintain all these different methods of tracking time, and the Romans prided themselves on organization. In fact, the use of different enumeration systems to mark the years in areas absorbed by the Romans was punishable by death as long as the Roman Empire was around.

By A.D. 525, however, the Roman Empire was a distant memory and the Church, which was the most enduring social structure of the day, thought that referencing some notable date in Christianity would be a better way of tracking time. In that year, a monk by the name of Dionysius Exiguus wrote *Cyclus Paschalis*, which was a history of events since the birth of Jesus. In this book, he uses A.D. 1 as the birth date of Jesus, and numbers later occurrences accordingly. This system of enumeration received the blessing of John I, the Pope at that time, and a couple of hundred years later, the Emperor Charlemagne made it the standard for secular affairs as well.

☞ IS ZERO NOTHING?

In most cases, zero designates a void or nothing. But when it comes to numbering years, the situation is a bit different. The calendar devised by Dionysius Exiguus moves directly from 1 B.C. to A.D. 1 without a "zero year." That means that if Jesus was born in 4 B.C. (see paragraph below) and died in A.D. 30, he would have been thirty-three years old, not thirty-four, at his crucifixion. The fact that there is no "zero year" means that all of you who cele-brated the beginning of a new millennium on January 1, 2000, jumped the gun by a year, although I doubt that many millennium parties considered the relationship between their soirees and the date of Jesus' birth.

WAS JESUS BORN BEFORE HIS BIRTH?

Since the time our friend Dionysius Exiguus established the tradi-tional year of Jesus' birth, strong evidence has indicated that one of the major players in the story of Jesus' birth, King Herod, died in 4 B.C. This means that Jesus could not have been born after that time. Thus, most scholars place the actual birth of Jesus some-where between 6 and 4 B.C.

Despite this consensus, no sane person has suggested shifting all the dates to make our numbering system correspond with this new information. However, some have argued that the confusion that would result from this is nothing compared to trying to ex-plain to a first-grade Sunday school class how Jesus was born sev-eral years prior to his birth. Contrary to the preceding paragraphs, then, all those who had their millennium party on January 1, 2000, were most likely a few years late. All this stuff makes it dicey to plan parties, doesn't it?

Anyway, this is the best we could do with B.C./A.D. Dr. Steve will leave it to others to straighten out the difference between AC/DC and AM/FM.

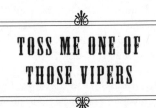

TOSS ME ONE OF
THOSE VIPERS

WARNING: Church Attendance Could Be Hazardous To Your Health. Especially if someone tosses a rattlesnake in your general direction during the closing hymn. To be sure, snake tossing is not likely to happen in most churches, but handling poisonous reptiles is practiced in about one hundred American congregations today. Snake handling derives from an interpretation of the so-called longer ending of Mark's Gospel, which reads, "And these signs will accompany those who believe: by using my name they will cast out demons; they will speak in new tongues; they will pick up snakes in their hands, and if they drink any deadly thing, it will not hurt them; they will lay their hands on the sick, and they will recover" (Mark 16:17-18).

THE BEGINNINGS OF SNAKE HANDLING

Snake handling got its start shortly after the Pentecostal movement began in the early twentieth century. With tongues speaking receiving so much attention, early Pentecostals couldn't help but notice the reference to speaking in tongues in Mark 16:17, which is followed immediately by a reference to handling serpents. For many, then, the logical conclusion is that if you speak in tongues, messing with snakes shouldn't be any problem.

By many accounts, snake handling started around 1908 when

George Went Hensley, a former bootlegger, was preaching on Mark 16 in a rural Tennessee church. In the middle of the sermon, some men from the congregation dumped a large box of rattlers in front of Hensley, who grabbed a handful of the slithering serpents and kept preaching. Dr. Steve is all for using visual aids in sermons, but this one seems a bit over the top. Nevertheless, this dramatic demo had the effect of kicking off a minor serpent-handling movement within Hensley's denomination, the Church of God, Cleveland, Tennessee. However, twenty years later, after a few people nearly died from snakebites, the denomination prohibited snake handling and revoked Hensley's preaching license, and the practice remained only in a few independent Appalachian churches.

In the 1940s, snake handling experienced something of a revival in the Church of God with Signs Following (which gets its name from the first part of Mark 16:17). Along with this resurgence came several deaths from snakebites. A number of southern states responded by passing laws prohibiting the practice, and Hensley himself, still playing with venomous critters, was arrested in Tennessee in 1947 under such a statute. Twenty-five years after Hensley's arrest, another snake-handling case wound up in Tennessee's state supreme court. In this case, the jurists decided that snake handling was not protected by the First Amendment and the ban was constitutional. Nevertheless, laws prohibiting snake handling are rarely enforced even though perhaps as many as one hundred deaths have occurred from snakebites (and a few from drinking poison) in churches, including one as recently as 2004.

SNAKE-HANDLING THEOLOGY

Since most churches that engage in serpent slinging are independent, there is no unified theology behind the practice. However, it usually is built around the idea that salvation involves three different levels—salvation, sanctification and baptism by the Holy Spirit. Only those who have experienced the last stage, Holy Spirit baptism, are thought to be protected against the poison of the snakes, so not everyone participates in this part of the worship, although they are present. The snakes are thought to be symbolic of Satan, and the ability to handle them without harm is viewed as a sign of an anointed believer's authority over the devil.

It should be noted that these reptiles are not treated gingerly. Rattlers, cottonmouths and vipers are often held three or four at a time in each hand, are thrown from one person to another, and are allowed to crawl around the neck and body. It's enough to give you the heebie-jeebies.

Of course, with this type of theological foundation, some confusion ensues when a snake handler gets bitten. Sometimes it is interpreted as a sign of sin in a person's life or evidence that he or she has not received the baptism of the Holy Spirit. In other cases, it is viewed as a time of testing, and those who experience the wrath of Satan's fangs rarely seek medical treatment. A third explanation, especially when a person dies, is that God has chosen that time to call a believer home. No doubt all three interpretations were considered on July 25, 1955, when George Went Hensley, the father of snake handling, died—from a rattlesnake bite.

☞ POSTSCRIPT: A RATTLESNAKE THEOLOGY OF PEOPLE HANDLING

As noted above, a significant number of people have died from fang punctures in religious services, and there are many more bites that don't lead to death (Hensley was reported to have been chomped by snakes about four hundred times). Nevertheless, the reckless handling of the venomous creatures has caused many to wonder why not even more snakebites occur. Some have theorized that the snakes are fed just prior to services to make them more docile, while others have said that they have been handled so often they are less likely to poke their fangs into folks.

Dr. Steve's research strongly suggests that the answer to this relative paucity of snakebites should be sought instead in the rattlesnake theology of human handling. Rattler doctrine views human beings as symbolic of Satan, as evidenced by the fact that whenever humans come in contact with venomous serpents, their first instinct is to bash the snake over the head with a heavy, blunt object. Thus, if a snake is able to handle people without getting bopped on its noggin, this is a sign of its authority over the devil. However, if a rattler's faith gets rattled while being flung hither and yon and resorts to biting a human, it is a sign that it is not truly anointed.

And now you know why snakebites occur infrequently in human-handling church services.

DID YOU KNOW?

The Puritans Who Stole Christmas

In 1659, Christmas became illegal in Puritan Massachusetts. Those who took the day off from work or celebrated with a feast on December 25 were liable to a fine of five shillings, the same amount that could be levied if caught gambling any day of the year. Under pressure from the English monarchy, the law revoking Christmas was itself revoked in 1687.

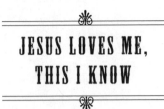

JESUS LOVES ME, THIS I KNOW

In American church life, probably no song is heard more frequently than "Jesus Loves Me." However, this simple song was not originally written as a hymn, but was part of a novel. What follows is the story of how words of comfort to a fictional dying child became the world's best-known Sunday school song.

The author of the verses for "Jesus Loves Me" was Anna Bartlett Warner (1820-1915). Her father was a prominent New York lawyer who suffered a severe financial setback in the depression of 1837. Nearly broke, he was forced to sell his New York townhouse and moved himself and his two daughters, Anna and Susan, to their summer home on Constitution Island, located on the Hudson River near the United States Military Academy at West Point.

To supplement the family income, Anna and Susan wrote, and were quite successful in publishing and selling their books, but not as successful at making money from them because of lax copyright laws. Susan's book *Wide, Wide World* is believed to have sold more copies in the mid-nineteenth century than any novel other than Harriet Beecher Stowe's *Uncle Tom's Cabin.* Some estimate that it was the first book by an American author to sell more than a million copies. Between the two sisters, they wrote over one hundred books, about a fifth of those as coauthors.

A SONG FOR A DYING CHILD

In 1860 Susan and Anna published a novel titled *Say and Seal.* In one scene, a young child named Johnny Fax is dying. Johnny is being held by Mr. Linden, his teacher, and asks to be comforted with a song. The words that follow were penned by Anna, and they appear here as they did in Mr. Linden's song for the dying child.

> Jesus loves me, this I know,
> For the Bible tells me so;
> Little ones to him belong;
> They are weak, but he is strong.
>
> Jesus loves me, he who died
> Heaven's gate to open wide;
> He will wash away my sin,
> Let his little child come in.
>
> Jesus loves me, loves me still,
> Though I'm very weak and ill;
> From his shining throne on high
> Comes to watch me where I lie.
>
> Jesus loves me, he will stay
> Close beside me all the way.
> Then his little child will take
> Up to heaven for his dear sake.

These words might well have been lost to history if not for Dr. William Bradbury. Bradbury was a prolific hymn writer, and provided the music for such familiar hymns as "He Leadeth Me" and "Just as I Am." In 1862 he set Anna Warner's words to music and added the well-known chorus:

> Yes, Jesus loves me!
> Yes, Jesus loves me!
> Yes, Jesus loves me! The Bible tells me so.

☞ THE WEST POINT CONNECTION

For fifty years, the Warner sisters, devout Christians, held Bible studies for the cadets at nearby West Point. Most of those years, the women would boat across the river to the military academy, but as they became too feeble, the cadets would come for their Bible classes at the Warner home on Constitution Island.

Susan, the older of the sisters, died in 1885, and Anna stayed on the island alone. Over the years she received some very attractive financial offers from developers who wanted to build an amusement park on Constitution Island. However, Anna's hope was that the island would become part of the West Point reservation. In 1908 she sold it at a much lower price to a philanthropist who then deeded the property to West Point, with the understanding that Anna could remain on Constitution Island for the remainder of her life. Anna died at the age of 95 in 1915. On her headstone are the words from one of her hymns, "We Would See Jesus."

> We would see Jesus, the great rock Foundation
> Whereon our feet were set with sovereign grace;
> Nor life nor death, with all their agitation,
> Can thence remove us, if we see His face.

As a sign of the West Point cadets' love for the Warner sisters, Susan and Anna are the only two civilians buried in the West Point Cemetery, with their graves located directly across the Hudson from Constitution Island.

☞ A "JESUS LOVES ME" POSTSCRIPT

Near the end of his life, the Swiss theologian Karl Barth made his first trip to America and engaged in a lecture tour that took him to this country's leading universities. Following one of these lectures, he was asked if he could sum up his theology in a short statement.

Barth, quite arguably the greatest theologian of the twentieth century and the author of literally thousands of erudite pages, thought a while and then gave his summary: "Jesus loves me, this I know, for the Bible tells me so."

From the greatest of theologians to the youngest child in the Sunday school, for almost a century and a half, the simple words of "Jesus Loves Me" keep bringing us back to the most profound truth of the Christian faith.

TATTOOS: THEY'RE NOT JUST FOR BIKERS ANYMORE

One of the hottest growth areas in retail business is tattooing. By some estimates, 15 percent of all Americans sport the permanent ink blot, and 25 percent of all those who fall into the twentysomething age group have one. Half of the new customers at tattoo parlors are female.

Perhaps even more surprisingly, a rapidly (and by some counts, the most rapidly) growing segment of the younger walking canvases are evangelical Christians. While tattoos were taboo in Christian circles a generation ago, that's all quickly changing. Many of the mostly college-age Christians seeking tattoos (or "tats," as the insiders call them) explain that they get them as a visible witness to their faith. So much for bumper stickers. Some will also admit that there's a little bit of rebellion in their decisions. Anecdotally, two of Dr. Steve's friends who teach biblical languages both report that they have had students ask them to write out stuff in Greek or Hebrew for the purpose of having it tattooed on their bodies (no indication was given about the intended location of said tattoos).

One sign that this is not just a small-scale fad is the CTA—the Christian Tattoo Association. This is a group of over one hundred tattoo artists, with a statement of purpose that asserts their aim "to spread the gospel to tattoo artists and enthusiasts" and "to promote health and safety issues in the field of tattooing and encourage moral and professional standards in the tattoo industry." Their online newsletter, *Eternal Ink*, gets thousands of hits a month.

For the little nippers and those who are a bit timid about a permanent tattoo, there are also temporary Christian tattoos. As the banner for one such manufacturer states, "The tattoo is temporary, the Truth is everlasting." So if you or your kid only want to make a three- to five-day commitment to a new "tat" (long enough, one advertiser notes, to memorize the inscribed Bible verse), the temporary versions are available from $1.50 and up (plus shipping and handling). And you will be pleased to know that all colors are FDA certified and nontoxic.

Obviously, this trend has not come without controversy. Many opponents point to the church's historical position on this issue. Early Christianity banned the practice up until about the tenth century. However, some of the Crusaders had themselves tattooed with the cross so they could be properly buried by the right group in the event of their demise in battle. In more recent years, some Christians have objected on the basis of "mark of the beast" or "defiling the 'temple of the Holy Spirit'" concerns.

Other warnings are of a more pragmatic nature, dealing with the permanence of the tattoo and the practice's earlier association with drunken sailors on leave and Harley riders.

Dr. Steve's theological guidance on the issue is that tattooing is probably safer for those who come from the "once saved, always saved" branch of Christianity. For Christians who aren't as big on the perseverance of the saints, more caution is advised. The smallest of tattoos begins at around thirty dollars, and bigger versions run into the thousand-dollar range. Tattoo removal begins at over a thousand. This means that the whole process of finding and losing your faith could start running into big bucks for tattooed, backsliding Nazarenes, not to mention more than a little physical discomfort (i.e., pain).

For many, the most quoted Scripture passage in the whole "to tattoo or not to tattoo" question is Leviticus 19:28, which states that "you shall not make any gashes in your flesh for the dead, or tattoo any marks upon you: I am the LORD." The "tattoo taboo" crowd views this injunction as sufficient justification for prohibiting the practice. On the other hand, the "do the tattoo" bunch from the Christian Tattoo Association lays out a rather lengthy *apologia* for the practice on their website. However, it ends with an interesting fallback position. "And if all else fails, just tell those critics of tattooing that Leviticus 19:28 states: 'You shall not . . . tattoo any marks on you'—this obviously means don't tattoo yourself, go to a professional!"

DID YOU KNOW?

The Reason People Have Middle Names

The person with the longest name in the Bible is Maher-shalal-hash-baz (Isaiah 8:1, 3). If the name isn't bad enough in itself, it means, "the spoil speeds, the prey hastens."

DUG UP

☞ THE CADAVER SYNOD

For some people, the fact that someone is dead just isn't quite good enough, and the Cadaver Synod is evidence that the basic absurdities of life can always be taken to new heights after life.

Pope Formosus died in 896 and was replaced by a pope who lasted less than a year. When the next pope, Stephen VI, ascended to the papacy in 897, he came into office nursing a long-standing grudge toward Formosus. The two had ended up on opposing sides in a political squabble, and Stephen apparently wasn't one to let dead and gones be bygones. Instead, he had the body of Pope Formosus, who had died a year earlier, dug up and placed on trial in what has come to be known as the Cadaver Synod.

During the trial, Formosus, or at least what was left of him, was dressed in full papal vestment and placed on a throne to face the charge that his appointment as pope was illegitimate since he already held another bishopric. Not surprisingly, Formosus had little to say in his own defense. Likewise, the deacon given the task of defending him did the politically wise thing and kept his own comments to a bare minimum while Pope Stephen VI hurled accusations and condemnations at the cadaver. When found guilty (was there any doubt?), the papal regalia was torn from Formosus's corpse, and the fingers of his right hand, from which he had dispensed priestly blessings, were cut off.

What happens next is a matter of some dispute. One account

says that the body was immediately thrown into the Tiber River. Another reports that he was buried in a common grave where he was again exhumed by grave robbers hoping to find something of value. When they discovered only a rotting body, they heaved it into the Tiber. In any case, Formosus's corpse was fished out downstream by a monk who buried it near Porto.

Pope Stephen may have been satisfied with his revenge, but his actions enraged the citizens of Rome. He was, in turn, arrested, thrown into prison and strangled to death. Stephen's successor, Pope Romanus, lasted only two months, and the next one, Pope Theodore II, lived a mere twenty days. However, during Ted II's reign, Formosus received a minor moral victory. Theodore II had Formosus exhumed again, transported from Porto to Rome, re-dressed in papal vestments and returned to his original tomb in St. Peter's. At last report, he's still there.

☞ WYCLIFFE AND ASSOCIATES

With John Wycliffe, we get an interesting series of connected characters who were dug up, or at least came close to it. Wycliffe was an English churchman in the fourteenth century who openly criticized the movement of the papacy from Rome to France during the Great Schism, as well as the immoral extravagances of the Holy See. He also won the hearts of many of his fellow Brits by attacking the papacy for its vast landholdings in England (it owned about one third of the property in England, all tax-exempt) and the taxes it imposed on that country's citizens. In addition, Wycliffe anticipated the ideas of the Reformation by rejecting the doctrines of purgatory, papal infallibility, transubstantiation and the selling of indulgences. He also got into hot water for translating Scripture into English.

Wycliffe was condemned by the pope for these activities, but was protected by the British nobility. He died of a stroke in 1384, before church officials could get their hands on him. However, they didn't forget about Wycliffe, because he trained a number of lay preachers, called the Lollards, who continued to preach his message of reform.

The traveling Lollards provide a connection with John Hus (sometimes Jan Huss), a scholar and priest from Bohemia. Hus was already acquainted with and favorable toward Wycliffe through the latter's philosophical writings. Persuaded by the preaching of the Lollards, who started showing up all over Bohemia, Hus eventually became an advocate of Wycliffe's reformist ideas. He was a powerful and influential preacher, and Hus soon had the church in Bohemia in an uproar, much to the pope's chagrin.

At first, Hus received the support of the Bohemian government, but the secular rulers received so much pressure from the papacy, which put Prague under an interdict (meaning that no religious services could be conducted in the city), that Hus was forced to retreat into the countryside. Hus was summoned to the Council of Constance to answer charges against him, but did not go until he received a promise of safe conduct, guaranteeing that he could return to Bohemia even if convicted.

Leaving the safety of his hometown, he traveled to Constance. After a month there, Hus was arrested on bogus charges and was held in pretty gruesome circumstances for months before being brought before the council. So much for safe passage. Hus was not allowed to speak in his defense at his "trial," where he was convicted of heresy and condemned to death by fire. He was stripped of his priestly robes and chained by the neck to a stake. The fire was set using Wycliffe's manuscripts as kindling. When it was all over, Hus's ashes were scooped up and thrown into the Rhine.

While there was no need for Hus to be dug up before being dumped in the river, there was still the festering matter of Wycliffe, who was viewed as the cause of this commotion. The same Council of Constance that executed Hus also declared Wycliffe a heretic. So now, more than thirty years after his death, the council demanded that Wycliffe's bones be dug up, burned, and the ashes tossed into the Swift River. They were. Take that, Wycliffe!

There is yet another reformist connection in this story. As Hus stood dying at the stake, he reportedly proclaimed that "in 100 years, God will raise up a man whose calls for reform cannot be suppressed." Hus was off by a couple of years. One hundred and two years later, in 1517, Luther nailed his Ninety-five Theses to the door of the Wittenberg Church, advocating many of the same things that Wycliffe and Hus had fought for. Luther himself lived out his natural life, but in 1547, a year after his death, he came close to suffering the same fate as Wycliffe. The armies of Charles V had conquered Wittenberg, and his soldiers wanted to exhume Luther's bones, burn them and throw them in the river. Charles declined, stating that he fought only against the living. Thus, Luther's remains remained in Wittenberg, but it was a close call. If nothing else, stories like this make you think twice about swimming in rivers.

ON A SOMEWHAT MORE POSITIVE NOTE

Not all religious exhumations were as rancorous as those above. Early in church history, the mortal remains of martyrs and other prominent Christians were often the objects of veneration (which is different from worship). In the middle of the second century, we hear of the faithful gathering up and preserving the bones of Polycarp, a church leader burned at the stake in one of the Roman persecutions. As Christians were given the right to construct church structures in the fourth century, they were frequently built over the graves of martyrs.

Early on, church leader prohibited the practice of digging up martyrs' graves to retrieve relics, but it still happened regularly. In fact, when St. Antony of Egypt was nearing death (which took a while since he lived to be 105 years old), he went into the desert with two associates and ordered them not to disclose the location of his grave lest his body be dug up and become the object of veneration. However, starting in the late sixth century, the process of canonization *required* that a prospective saint's remains be exhumed prior to beatification so that they might be divided up (*partitioned* is the official term) and divvied out to various churches as relics. In this case, then, being dug up postmortem is a compliment, although I'm not certain most of these saints would like being called a relic.

THE GIDEONS

The United States has about 3.5 million hotel rooms. So what will you find in almost every one of them? If you said a Magic Fingers vibrating massage mattress, you would be wrong, and probably older than you want to admit. The real answer is that you will discover a Bible tucked away in a drawer somewhere, with the words "Placed by the Gideons" stamped on the cover.

Gideons International, the organization responsible for the Bible in your motel room, was named after the Old Testament Gideon. Ironically, however, since many Gideon Bibles are the New Testament with Proverbs and the Psalms and do not include the full Old Testament, you won't be able to read about the namesake of the group in their own Bible. In any case, Gideons was chosen as the name of the group because the Old Testament Gideon was willing to do whatever God wanted him to do, even though seriously understaffed (Judges 6–7). More than a hundred years after their founding, Gideons International has about 250,000 members in almost one hundred countries, a slightly larger army than the original Gideon had. They now place more than sixty million Bibles, in over eighty languages, annually.

☞ Did You Hear the One About Three Traveling Salesmen?

All this comes from rather unlikely beginnings. In 1898, John Nicholson, a traveling salesman from Janesville, Wisconsin, was looking for a hotel room while on the road. When he tried to check into the Central Hotel in Boscobel, Wisconsin, he discovered that all the rooms were taken. Arrangements were made for Nicholson to share a room with Samuel Hill, another traveling salesman, from Beloit, Wisconsin.

As they visited that evening, Nicholson and Hill both acknowledged the need for a fellowship group for Christian business travelers. The following year, the two men met at the Janesville YMCA with a third traveling salesman, W. J. Knights. Together, the three formed the "Christian Commercial Travelers' Association of America" as a fellowship for "Christian traveling men of the world" and to help put an end to all the unsavory traveling salesman jokes.

☞ Into the Hotel Room and Beyond

From these humble beginnings, the Gideons grew rather quickly. By 1908 there were seven thousand members, mostly commercial travelers. The idea came up that having Bibles available in hotel reception areas would be helpful so guests could borrow one while on the road. From here, it was suggested that they be placed directly in each room, and the organization unanimously resolved to make that their goal. The first order came from a hotel in Montana for twenty-five Bibles.

Since then, the Gideons have also focused on making the Bible available in doctors' offices and hospitals and placed Bibles with the military, emergency responders, firefighters, law enforcement personnel, and, on the other side of the law enforcement equation, in jails and prisons. Distribution of the Scriptures in schools and universities began in 1946. The Gideons Auxiliary, made up of the wives of Gideon members, also makes white Bibles available to nurses and in nursing programs.

☞ GIVING BIBLES AWAY IS NOT AS EASY AS IT USED TO BE

The Gideons' work has met increasing challenges in recent years. In 1953 the Supreme Court ruled that Bible distribution by Gideons in public schools was unconstitutional, although this ruling was ignored by school districts for many years. In fact, if Dr. Steve had known the Bible he received from the Gideons in his public school as a fifth grader was contraband, he probably would have been more inclined to read it back then. Many districts work around this by making Bibles available within the school to be picked up voluntarily by students, but even this has been challenged in court. Recently the Borgata Hotel and Casino in Atlantic City refused to allow placement of Gideon Bibles in its new two-thousand-room hotel, citing fears of offending its diverse customer base.

On the other side of things, many other groups have noted the Gideons' achievements and, in a case of "success invites imitation," have started placing their own books in hotels. Thus, depending on where you check in, you might find drawer-mates for the Gideon Bible such as *The Teaching of Buddha, The Book of Mormon* or, from the Scientologists, a little book by L. Ron Hubbard titled *The Way to Happiness.* The Scientologists are still behind the Gideons in U.S. hotel placements by about 3.4 million.

STILL GOING STRONG

Despite these challenges, the Gideons International continues to give away 120 Bibles per minute. Most are King James Versions of the New Testament with Psalms and Proverbs; however, Gideons also distribute the Scriptures in the Berkley Version for placement in Roman Catholic schools and hospitals (although Catholics are not permitted membership in the Gideons). The cost of the Gideons' most common version of Scripture is about $1.50, and it is financed by bequests, contributions and church offerings. All administrative costs for the organization are paid from member dues. More than 90 percent of the funds received by the Gideons goes directly to printing and placement of Bibles. The average life expectancy of a Gideon Bible in a hotel room is about seven years.

So the next time you are in a hotel room, take some time to open the drawer and pull out the Gideon Bible. Drop a quarter in the Magic Fingers vibrating massage machine, plop down on the bed, and spend some time in the Scriptures. If nothing else, it will make you think twice before checking out with a Holiday Inn towel stuffed in your suitcase.

IN SEARCH OF
THE HOLY GRAIL

Most of us know that how hard it is to find a lost item even when you know exactly what you are looking for, and possibly even know exactly where you left it. The job becomes exponentially more difficult when you are searching for a lost item and you are not even certain what that something is.

☞ WHAT IS THE HOLY GRAIL?

Perhaps that's why, after centuries of searching, no one has ever been able to locate the Holy Grail, an object that is described in a wide variety of ways. A group of Crusaders from Genoa paid a huge price for an emerald chalice reputed to be the Grail, although it was dropped during the nineteenth century and discovered to be green glass instead of emerald, a bit too late to ask for a refund. The Holy Grail has also been represented as a large gem, a stone, a book, a platter, an agate cup, a two-handled silver chalice, a Celtic cauldron and, more recently in *The Da Vinci Code*, the mortal remains, or what remains of the remains, of Mary Magdalene (who the book portrays as the wife of Jesus). Confusion about the Grail probably explains why nowhere in the entirety of *Monty Python and the Holy Grail* does it show the object of those brave knights' quest.

☞ THE GRAIL IN MEDIEVAL LITERATURE

No written record of the Holy Grail's existence can be found in the first several centuries of the church's history, and it has never had a place in Eastern Christianity. However, it becomes a hot topic in later medieval literature, where it is strongly linked with the stories of King Arthur and his Camelot cronies. Chretien de Troyes penned what many consider to be the earliest of the Grail stories, the oldest section being written at the end of the twelfth century. In this story, Perceval visits the Grail Castle, where he views a procession that includes a bleeding lance and a *graal*, or platter, with a head on it. Perceval had been told prior to his visit that he should mind his manners and not inquire as to the meaning of these strange things. Ironically, this was one of the very few times when keeping one's mouth shut at a party turned out to be lousy advise, since Perceval's questioning would have brought about the healing of his host and his entire kingdom.

While Chretien's version ascribes no direct religious significance to the *graal*, Robert de Boron's version adds new elements that draw the legend into the history of the church. In de Boron's work, the *graal* is the dish used by Jesus in the Last Supper. This platter came into the possession of Joseph of Arimathea and was used to catch the blood of Jesus when he was removed from the cross. The lance in Chretien's tale is represented as the weapon that pierced Jesus' side when he was on the cross.

The Joseph of Arimathea connection becomes the link to the idea of the Grail Castle. In the legend, the Jewish authorities reward Joseph for providing both comfort and a tomb for Jesus by imprisoning him in a stone tomb. While Joseph is left there to rot, the risen Jesus appears to him and gives him the grail, which miraculously gives him nourishment for years until he was released. As the story goes, Joseph heads to Britain, and the grail is handed down to and protected by his descendants, including the lame

Fisher King who lives in the Grail Castle when questers show up in search of the Grail.

As the medieval period continues, the identity of the knights seeking the Grail changes. Sometimes it is Perceval, Gawain, Lancelot or Galahad. Some variations of the story portray the quest as ending in failure, as is the case for Lancelot because of his sexual dalliances, and later, for Sir Robin the Not-Quite-so-Brave-as-Sir-Lancelot in Monty Python's version. In other cases, the search is successful. Gawain and Galahad fall into the latter category, and in one account, a herd of twelve knights ascends into heaven with the Grail itself. One enduring variation of the story has the Holy Grail coming into the possession of the Knights Templar, a group also reputed to have once guarded the Shroud of Turin.

◄ THE REVIVAL OF THE GRAIL

The folks of the Renaissance were not quite as deep into knights, chivalry and questing as their medieval counterparts, so the Grail story died out for several centuries. However, interest in the Holy Grail got a new infusion of life in late nineteenth-century Romanticism with Wagner's operatic *Parsifal* and Tennyson's *Idylls of the King*. Hollywood also picked up the torch with several cinematic adaptations. Among them, *The Light of Faith* (1922) featured Lon Chaney, and *The Silver Chalice* was Paul Newman's first acting gig. The Holy Grail also plays into *Indiana Jones and the Last Crusade*. However, it is common consensus that *Monty Python and the Holy Grail* provides the definitive cinematic presentation on the theme.

WE DO IT ALL FOR YOU®

The term *megachurch* usually refers to congregations with an average attendance of more than two thousand people each week, so a church with twelve thousand members and seven thousand in Sunday school each week would easily qualify. However, it might be more appropriate to refer to Brentwood Baptist Church as a "super-sized-church," because it is the only congregation in the world (so far) with its own McDonald's® franchise.

The wheels began to turn when Brentwood's senior pastor, Joe Samuel Ratliff, attended a conference for black operators of McDonald's® franchises. Since their restaurants are already in airports, hospitals, museums and virtually everywhere else, he asked why none had been located on a church campus. Discussions soon led to the first ever McDonald's® franchise in a church.

So now, after a couple of hours of hoops on Brentwood's NBA®-regulation-size basketball court, you can mosey down the hall of the 74,000-square-foot Joe Samuel Ratliff Lifelong Learning Center, look for the Golden Arches® (they do have Arches®) and recharge with a Super Value Meal®. Too busy to go inside? Have it your way® (oops, that doesn't sound quite right). There is also a drive-through window for those who may be headed to the Family Christian Center in Munster, Indiana, a "venti-sized church" that has its own Starbucks® coffee franchise.

LOTS OF WIVES, A BUNCH OF EXECUTIONS AND A BOOK (EPISODE I)

On occasion, we hear about book burning, but it is not often we hear of someone being burned because of a book. That's kind of what happened to Thomas Cranmer.

ALL I WANTED TO DO WAS BE A SCHOLAR

Things started quietly enough for Cranmer. Born in 1489, he attended Cambridge and was given a fellowship at Jesus College when he finished his B.A. However, he fell in love with and married the daughter of a local tavern-owner and had to relinquish his teaching post, which came with a celibacy clause. His wife died a few years later during childbirth, so he returned to his fellowship and became a priest.

What looked like the beginning of a peaceful academic life soon took on soap-opera proportions. Cranmer caught the attention of King Henry VIII when two of his aides discovered that Cranmer supported the king's quest to have his marriage to Catherine of Aragon annulled. Catherine's fault was that she seemed incapable of providing Henry with a male heir to the throne (although she had produced a daughter, Mary), and the king feared that civil war would ensue should he die without an heir. Cranmer was sent as part of a delegation to plead Henry's case before the pope. When this did not prove successful, Henry started a series of church reforms that reduced the English church's commitment to Rome and gave the king significant ecclesiastical power. Henry, however, had no intention of breaking away from Catholicism.

The pope actually had theological grounds for granting an annulment since Catherine was the widow of Henry's brother, so the marriage was actually contrary to church law in the first place. The sticking point was that Catherine was the aunt of Charles V, emperor of the Holy Roman Empire. Despite the old saying about how this political structure was neither holy, Roman nor an empire, Charles V's armies packed enough wallop to sack Rome. The fact that the pope's security was now in Charles's hands assured that he would not annul the marriage.

Cranmer, in a fateful move, was sent to the Holy Roman Empire as the British ambassador in 1532. There he spent considerable time with the Lutheran scholar Osiander and took a strong liking both to his theology (not exactly acceptable behavior for a Catholic priest) and to his niece, whom he married (definitely unacceptable for a Catholic priest).

🔖 MEANWHILE, BACK IN JOLLY OLD ENGLAND

Henry's need for a divorce had now become urgent because the woman he desired to marry, Anne Boleyn, was pregnant. The two were secretly married, even though Henry was still officially wed to Catherine. Two months later, an opportunity arose for Henry VIII to clean up the books a bit; the archbishop of Canterbury, the highest church official in England, died. Henry appointed Cranmer to the post, knowing that he would declare his marriage to Catherine null and void and sanctify the marriage to Anne Boleyn. Cranmer complied.

None of this maneuvering resolved the king's heir-loss problems, however. Anne Boleyn's child turned out to be another girl, Elizabeth, and after two subsequent miscarriages, Cranmer annulled this marriage. Anne B. was arrested on trumped-up charges of adultery and beheaded. Cranmer later invalidated Henry's subsequent marriages to Anne of Cleves (who was given the title of "King's Sister" and Anne Boleyn's old castle for her brief services), Catherine Howard (also beheaded for adultery) and maybe even Elizabeth Taylor, although historians are divided on that one.

The one bright spot in all this is that wife number three, Jane Seymour (tucked in between Anne B. and Anne C.), did produce a son, Edward. Unfortunately for her, she died in childbirth. Henry VIII married one last time, to Catherine Parr, who managed to outlive him. For those of you keeping score, it was three "Catherines," two "Annes" and a "Jane."

While Cranmer allowed significant latitude to Henry VIII in all matters matrimonial, Henry VIII didn't exactly reciprocate. The king, who wanted the English church to stay Catholic but under his control rather than the pope's, didn't approve of clerical marriage. So Cranmer was forced to keep his wife from public view for years, and she was later banished for a time by Henry.

☞ THE KING (HENRY VIII) IS DEAD; LONG LIVE THE KID, I MEAN, KING (EDWARD VI)

When Henry VIII died in 1547, he left a real mess. After six wives, (insert five golden rings), four divorces, three royal children (each calling a different woman "mommy"), two spousal executions and one married archbishop, you know things are going to be messy for the next king, especially if he happens to be only ten years old when he ascends to the throne.

So now you have a bunch of ticked-off powerful people, a kid-king and a rather befuddled (and married, if that's not redundant with "befuddled") leader of a national church in the throes of major turmoil. It's safe to say that you can count on a few more executions. Who will it be? Tune in to the next episode of "Lots of Wives, a Bunch of Executions and a Book" on page 150.

DID YOU KNOW?

Thanks for Leading the Great Awakening. You're Fired!

Many know of Jonathan Edwards as one of America's preeminent theologians and philosophers. Others are aware of his pivotal role as a preacher in the Great Awakening, which spread revival throughout New England. Even with all this fame, Edwards was not bulletproof. He was fired from his pastorate at Northampton Church, a large and prestigious congregation he had served for almost twenty-five years, over his handling of church discipline. The ecclesiastical council voted to dismiss him, and the congregation ratified the decision, with only twenty-three voting in favor of Edwards and more than two hundred against.

MOTTOS

Every group needs a catchy line to quickly and effectively communicate something important about the organization. Christian organizations are no different. See if you can match the motto to the appropriate Christian denomination or institution. (See pages 159-60 for the answers.)

1. Azusa Pacific University

a. Earnestly Contending for the Faith

2. United Church of Christ

b. Where the Scriptures speak, we speak; where the Scriptures are silent, we are silent.

3. Salvation Army

c. God First, Since 1899

4. Christian Church (Disciples of Christ)

d. Win the Campus for Christ Today, Win the World for Christ Tomorrow

5. University of Notre Dame

e. That they may all be one

6. United Methodist Church

f. Blood and Fire

7. American Council of Christian Churches

g. Open Hearts. Open Minds. Open Doors.

8. Baylor University

h. *Pro Ecclesia, Pro Texana* (For Church, For Texas)

9. Holt International

i. *Crux spes unica* (The cross is the only hope)

10. Campus Crusade for Christ

j. Every child deserves a home.

☛ POSTSCRIPT ON INSTITUTIONAL MOTTOS

Perhaps those who despair of institutions not grounded in Christian faith will find affirmation of their fear in the motto of the University of British Columbia. Inscribed on the university's coat of arms are two Latin words, *Tuum est*, which can either be translated as "It is yours" or "It's up to you." We assume the latter translation does not apply to correct answers on final exams at the school.

☛ POSTSCRIPT ON LATIN INSTITUTIONAL MOTTOS

If a group really wants to show some academic muscle, they get a jump-start by using Latin. One motto just screaming to be adopted by some institution is "I hear, I see, I learn," or rendered in the more sophisticated Latin, *Audio, Video, Disco.* Sounds custom-made for a college that needs some marketing help.

SEARCHIN' FOR STRAYS

You city slickers may think you have all the ministry angles covered, but I'll bet there's one you haven't even thought of yet. Don't worry, though, a lot of good folks are already taking care of it. Yep, it's rodeo ministry, perhaps the only type of ministry where a website will greet you with "Howdy and Hallelujah."

The first thing you need to know about Christian rodeo is that it is not some small-potatoes operation. One rodeo ministry, the FCC (that's the Fellowship of Christian Cowboys, not the Federal Communications Commission), is on its way toward a hundred chapters operating all across the U.S. These groups are dedicated to fusing the gospel message with the cowboy and rodeo worlds. Whether you are looking for Christian rodeo announcers, Christian rodeo clowns (to schedule one such clown, you are advised to contact Mike or Bubba), or are in search of pre- or post-rodeo cowboy preachers, you can find the right hired hands as you go "searchin' for strays," as one rodeo ministry site puts it. There is even a Christian rodeo circuit.

If you are wondering whether the kids will be left out, you will be happy to know that your yearlings can take their pick from over twenty-five rodeo Bible camps each year. These camps combine instruction on various rodeo events with other Christian camping activities. Cowpokes nine years old and up can hone their skills in breakaway roping, bull riding, goat tying, team roping, horsemanship (for the latter you will likely need to supply your own snaffle bit or bosal) and other events. They can even learn how to improve their times in the steer undecorating event. (Given that a steer already gets undecorated on the way to becoming a steer, any further undecorating hardly sounds like a very Christian thing to do to a steer.) These camps for aspiring cowboys and cowgirls are offered all across the country from Montana to Kansas (sponsored by the Cowboys at the Cross Chapter) to Florida, although they don't seem to have made it to Massachusetts yet.

Still not convinced that Christian rodeo is the real deal? Then you should know it has the two primary indicators of a bona fide Christian subculture. First, Christian rodeo has its own designed-just-for-them Bible, the *Cowboy Bible* (NASB). The second clear sign that Christian rodeo has arrived is that it has its own bumper stickers. More accurately, it has its own decals for the back window of a pickup. This manufacturer clearly knows its market. Whether you want the barrel-racer version of the cowgirl kneeling before the cross, the team-roping "ropin' on faith" sticker or versions that allow you to personalize your own message, these decals remind us that Christian rodeo is going to stick with us for a while.

If rodeo really isn't your thing, the "Mission: Rodeo Christian Ministries" website is kind enough to provide a link to the "Christian Surfers United States" website.

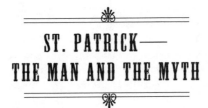

ST. PATRICK—
THE MAN AND THE MYTH

About the only things that most people connect with the name St. Patrick are green beer and strategically placed pinches. A few know some of the legends that have sprung up around the man behind the March seventeenth holiday, but these are mostly blarney. While St. Paddy is credited with driving the snakes out of Ireland, the truth is that there probably never were any snakes there in the first place. Moreover, it is doubtful that he ever explained the mysteries of the Trinity by using a shamrock as a teaching prop. However, St. Patrick is one of those rare individuals whose real life is even more impressive than the myths that have been attached to him.

☛ SLAVERY

Patrick, or Patricius by his given name, was born around 415, the son of a rather prominent Roman family living in Briton (now Great Britain). Even though this region had been part of the Roman Empire, the Roman legions had been pulled back to protect Rome from the barbarians. This left Briton vulnerable to attacks from invaders from Ireland. During one such attack, Patrick, who was about sixteen at the time, was taken prisoner, sent to Ireland and sold as a slave. He was put in charge of tending pigs and treated very poorly, constantly living on the verge of starvation.

Patrick, who had been at best a nominal Christian prior to his enslavement, used his long stretches of isolation to get back in touch with God and was constantly in prayer. After six years of slavery, he received a vision in which a voice told him that he would return to his homeland and that a ship was waiting for him. So Patrick escaped and did find his ship, although he had to walk two hundred miles to get to it (the vision didn't tell him about that part of the deal).

☞ FREEDOM

After a three-day voyage, Patrick ended up in what is now France. The details of the years that followed are foggy, but it seems probable that he spent some time studying at a monastery in France. He was eventually ordained as a priest and returned to Briton. Here he received a second vision, which he tells us about in his *Confessions,* a brief autobiography that has survived the ages. In it, an Irishman named Victoricius comes to him with a handful of letters. He hands one of the letters to Patrick, which begins with the words, "The voice of the Irish." When he reads these words, Patrick hears voices calling for him to bring the gospel to Ireland. From that moment on, he knows he has to return.

☞ BACK TO IRELAND

Fifth-century Ireland was a pretty nasty place. As we saw earlier in our story, various tribes frequently invaded neighboring lands, and when they weren't invading other regions, they were constantly at war with each other. Slavery was a common practice, and human sacrifice was practiced in their religion. Prior to Patrick's arrival, a bishop named Palladius had been sent to Ireland to evangelize a region that had been completely untouched by Christianity. He either died en route or was quickly martyred once he arrived. Regardless of his actual fate, Ireland was a thoroughly pagan and brutal place when Patrick returned as bishop to this country he had last seen as a slave.

During his enslavement, Patrick had acquired fluency in the Celtic language and knowledge of the cultural and religious practices, which proved invaluable as he sought to evangelize this land. However, it was tough sledding as he sought to make inroads with the Irish. In his *Confessions*, he speaks frequently of threats to his life, coming mostly from druid priests who did not take kindly to the idea of giving up any religious turf to Christianity.

Legends abound about contests between Patrick and the druids in which Patrick's victories would win over kings to the Christian faith. While the details of his evangelistic methods are lost to us, it is clear that Patrick would appeal to the various tribal leaders. If you converted the king, you also got his subjects. As various groups embraced Christianity, Patrick would plant monasteries and convents to carry on the work. He would then quickly move on to bring the message of Christ to a new area of the country.

☞ PATRICK'S LEGACY

At his death (sometime around 493), almost all of Ireland had been evangelized, and monasteries dotted the countryside. As continental Europe was overrun by the barbarians in the following decades and centuries, these monasteries were instrumental in preserving the documents of the past and the tradition of Christian learning—an educational legacy that's somewhat ironic given Patrick's insecurities about his own educational deficiencies. Patrick's example also spawned an amazing missionary zeal among Irish monks, who soon spread out all over Europe with the gospel. Another lasting memorial to the influence of Patrick was the abolition of slave trading in Ireland shortly after his death. In an age where the church tolerated the practice, Patrick, no doubt remembering his own slavery, spoke out clearly and strongly against it.

Many of the specific details of Patrick's life have been lost to the past, but what is undeniable is that this humble and courageous individual changed the history of an entire country. Somebody ought to have a parade. Wonder why no one has thought of that?

WHO NAMED THIS DENOMINATION ANYWAY?

For better or worse, the U.S. has thousands of different denominational groups. This makes the odds pretty high that you will find a few groups with names that induce vigorous head-scratching. All the names below are actual names of honest-to-goodness denominations. For those Baptists who feel like they are being picked on below, just remember, y'all have more denominations than all the other church families combined.

If one starts from a particular perspective, some denominational names sound downright oxymoronic. Loosen up a bit and try the list below for a few that might fit this category:

☞ OXYMORONIC DENOMINATIONAL NAMES?

- Orthodox Presbyterians
- Salvation Army
- United Methodists
- Free Methodists
- Regular Baptists
- Charismatic Episcopal Church
- Evangelical Free
- Reformed Baptists
- Progressive Baptists
- Fundamental Methodist Conference Fellowship of Independent Evangelical Churches

The winner in the category for a possible double oxymoron: **United Free Will Baptists.**

Honorable mention:
After a split from the Southern Baptist Convention in 1991, a new group named itself the **Cooperative Baptist Fellowship.**

While some denominational names tend toward oxymorons, others seem a bit redundant. For example:

☞ REDUNDANT DENOMINATIONAL NAMES?

- Primitive Baptists
- Strict Baptists
- Old Catholic Church
- Independent Baptists
- Byzantine Catholics

- Protestant Reformed
- Separate Baptists
- Conservative Mennonite Conference
- Independent Fundamental Churches of America

Redundancy category winner, awarded by the Redundancy Department of Redundancy: **General Association of General Baptists.**

☛ BOTH REDUNDANT AND OXYMORONIC?

- The Separate Baptists in Christ

☛ DENOMINATIONAL NAMES THAT MAKE YOU GO "HUH?"

- Church of God with Signs Following
- Two-Seed-in-the-Spirit Predestinarian Baptist
- Interstate and Foreign Landmark Missionary Baptist Association
- Assemblies of the Called Out Ones of Yah

DID YOU KNOW?

It Was Probably Over Budget Too

It is not unusual for major construction projects to drag out beyond their scheduled completion dates, but the cathedral of Cologne, Germany, takes this tendency to extremes. The foundation stone for the new cathedral was laid in August 1248. However, the cathedral was not completed until 1880. Despite a construction period of more than six hundred years, the completed church kept to the original master design.

COLUMBA

You would think people would know better than to argue about the rightful ownership of a single copy of a book. Sure it all starts small, but you start fighting over a book and the next thing you know you end up with a battle where hundreds of people are killed, Scotland gets evangelized, and you have the first recorded sighting of the Loch Ness Monster. Just in case we haven't learned our lessons, though, here's the story of Columba.

☞ IT'S MINE! NO, IT'S MINE!

Columba was an Irish priest who was granted access to the scriptorium of Finnian to copy a Psalter. Columba assumed he would be allowed to keep the copy when he was done; Finnian did not share that assumption. The ownership dispute led to the Battle of Cul Dreimhne (561), resulting in the deaths of numerous soldiers on both sides. When the smoke had cleared, Columba still believed the manuscript was rightfully his, but felt really rotten about how things had spiraled out of control. His confessor said that a fitting penance would be what has come to be called "white martyrdom"—self-exile to a mission field.

He didn't have far to go to find a mission

field. Heading off in a small boat with eleven other monks, he went to Scotland, the island of Iona to be exact. The band of monks built a monastery on the island and used it as a base for establishing additional monasteries and schools as well as evangelizing the heathen Picts on the mainland.

 NESSIE AS EVANGELISTIC TOOL

As legend has it, on one foray into mainland Scotland to meet with a Pictish king in 565, Columba came across some men burying a friend who had been killed by a sea monster. Seeing another swimmer also being threatened by the monster, he raised his cross and commanded that the beast retreat. When the big critter complied with Columba's order, several Picts converted on the spot. This is the first recorded sighting of the Loch Ness Monster in history, with the next Nessie appearance not occurring until 1933. This is obviously one very old monster.

Though Columba never returned to his native Ireland after this self-imposed exile, he is considered, along with St. Patrick and St. Brigid, one of Ireland's three patron saints. Nevertheless, he is still honored in Scotland, and some credit him with the introduction of whiskey to the country. Whether true or not, Scotland produces a crème whiskey named after him still today. It reportedly goes well with haggis.

The moral of the story: next time you have a copyright argument, just keep in mind the law of unintended consequences.

CHAPTER AND VERSE

Did you know that John 3:16 was not in Bibles until about 1550? I'm not talking about the "For God so loved the world that he gave his only Son . . ." part. That was in there. What those earlier Bibles were missing were the chapter and verse designations that help you find this particular passage in Scripture. So where did these come from?

☞ A NEW CHAPTER IN CHAPTERS

The inclusion of chapter and verse markers is part of a bigger story about how the production of written materials has changed. Prior to the printing press, everything was copied by hand, a time-consuming and expensive process. Even the materials used for writing were pricey. To save money, the earliest manuscripts of Scripture we possess were in what is called *scriptio continua;* there were no spaces between the words, sentences and paragraphs, and no punctuation. It was thrifty, but made reading a bit difficult.

Jewish scholars introduced something like verse divisions in the Hebrew Scriptures around A.D. 200. Because most Jews during this age spoke Aramaic rather than Hebrew, a portion of Scripture in Hebrew (usually about a sentence in length) would be read, and then the same section would be read in Aramaic. Later these divisions were indicated by a *soph pasuq*, which looks like a colon (the punctuation type of colon, not an intestine).

The chapter designations that we are familiar with today were inserted into the Vulgate—the Latin translation used during the medieval period—by Stephen Langton, who later became the archbishop of Canterbury, in 1205.

☞ THEN WE GET THE VERSES

Three hundred and fifty years after Langton, the system and numbering of verses we now use was added to his chapter divisions. This versification was provided by Estienne (sometimes referred to by the Latinized version of his name, Robert Stephanus), a printer from Paris. For the verses of the Old Testament, Estienne relied on the location of the *soph pasuq* in the Hebrew versions. Wherever there was a *soph pasuq*, he removed it and simply inserted a number in its place. His versification of the New Testament was another matter completely. Estienne devised the numbering of verses within the New Testament chapters while riding his horse between Paris and Lyons. When you look at some of the places where verses begin and end in the New Testament, you gather it must have been a pretty rough ride.

Estienne first used this system of versification in a Greek-Latin New Testament published in 1551, and later used the same numbering in a French translation of the Bible in 1553. The first complete English-language Bible to employ Estienne's versification was the Geneva Bible (the Bible used by William Shakespeare and John Bunyan) in 1560. As a side note, the Geneva Bible is often referred to also as the "Breeches Bible." In Genesis 3:7, after Adam and Eve have eaten the forbidden fruit and realized they were naked, the Geneva Bible says "they sewed fig tree leaves together, and made themselves breeches" (an old form of the word "britches").

It never hurts to remember that the system of chapters and verses was not originally part of the Bible and that these divisions don't always provide the best guidance on how the various sections fit together as literary units. However, since it does not look like the current numbering of chapters and verses will go away any time soon, you might like to know that there are 1,189 chapters in the Bible (929 in the Old Testament, 260 in the New Testament) and a total of 31,173 verses (23,214 in the Old Testament, 7,959 in the New Testament).

NOT YOUR ORDINARY THIEVING EVANGELIST

The most famous American evangelist of the early twentieth century was a thief. This isn't rumor or innuendo. The evangelist himself admitted it—with pride. If you don't believe it, there is even an official record of the times he was caught, but all the records agree that he got away with stealing more often than he got nailed.

The evangelist's name was Billy Sunday. Sunday's father was a Yankee soldier during the Civil War who died of pneumonia a month after Billy was born. His widow, left alone in a two-room log cabin in Iowa, struggled to keep her two sons fed, but eventually had to send them to a soldier's orphanage. Billy didn't care much for the orphanage and ran away to his grandfather's farm. He decided he didn't like farming much either and ran away from there as well. He later worked his way through high school as a janitor.

☞ THE BIRTH OF AN EVANGELIST

A few years later, Billy Sunday, now married, was doing Christian outreach work for a YMCA in Iowa. Money was tight on his $83 per month salary, and Sunday received financial relief when he got an offer to work as an advance man for J. Wilbur Chapman, an evangelist of some fame in the Midwestern state. This experience with the inner workings of evangelistic crusades proved valuable. Eventually, however, Chapman took a church on the East Coast, but was still scheduled to do one last crusade in Garner, Iowa. Chapman gave Sunday his seven sermons, and Sunday preached the meetings himself.

The gig in Garner went so well that Billy received invitations to do more in other cities. His crusades grew larger, and soon his reputation took him beyond the Midwest crusade circuit. In 1901 he hired a song leader who worked with him for the next twenty years, and Sunday's own unique style began to take shape. At each crusade location, a tabernacle was constructed, sometimes capable of seating up to twenty thousand, with sawdust on the floor to keep the dust down. Thus, we discover the origin of the phrase "hitting the sawdust trail," which describes the penitent's trip to the tabernacle altar to find salvation at the service's conclusion. And they came. It was estimated that Sunday preached to one hundred million people during his career.

☞ HOW A THIEF BECAME AN EVANGELIST

By Billy Sunday's own admission, he was a fairly marginal preacher when he started. So how do we account for his broad success as an evangelist? Part of it was his unassuming personality. He had a charisma that made him immediately likeable, and his Midwestern upbringing allowed him to connect with his audience. Some of his success can be attributed his antics. Sunday was an animated preacher who started in a suit and usually ended without a coat and tie and with his shirtsleeves rolled up. He also knew how to get publicity and was once rumored to have hired a giant from the Barnum and Bailey Circus as an usher for one of his crusades. But the biggest publicity plug came from Sunday's own reputation as a thief.

🔖 BILLY'S THIEVING DAYS

While Billy Sunday was working his way through high school as a janitor, he developed a rather solid regional reputation as a baseball player. When Cap Anson, considered by many to be professional baseball's first superstar, came to town, he was introduced to Sunday. Anson was now a scout for his old team, the Chicago White Stockings (which became the Chicago Cubs, not the White Sox), and didn't really think Sunday had what it took to go pro. His mind quickly changed when he put Billy up against the White Stockings' fastest player. Billy whupped him by fifteen feet in a hundred-yard race, and Anson signed him to a contract right there.

Sunday's professional baseball career did not exactly get off to a flying start; he struck out in his first thirteen at bats. However, Sunday eventually got the hang of big league pitching and ended up with a lifetime batting average of .248, with a career-high average of .291 during the 1887 campaign with the White Stockings. While .248 is not exactly the gold standard of averages for an outfielder, Sunday made up for it on the base paths. Once on base, he was all but unstoppable. Rickey Henderson set the major-league record in 1982 with 130 stolen bases, but that was in 162 games.

During the 1890 season, his last year as a professional player, Sunday had 84 stolen bases in 117 games. He was the first major leaguer to get around the bases in under fourteen seconds. Billy's biggest problem as a player was that you cannot steal first base.

☞ FROM THE STADIUM TO THE TABERNACLE

Professional baseball players at the end of the nineteenth century were a rough-and-tumble bunch, and Billy fit in well. During his fourth season, he and some fellow White Stockings were hitting the bottle pretty hard, their usual form of post-game recreation, when a hymn-playing band from the Pacific Garden Mission came by. Their music reminded Billy of a song his mother used to sing, so he went with them to the mission and came to faith. Sunday soon became active in a church and started speaking at YMCAs. He wasn't much for talking in front of groups at that stage of his life, but his reputation as terror on the base paths kept people in their seats.

Sunday remained in professional baseball for another four years after his conversion, but in 1891 he turned down a contract from the Philadelphia Athletics. Instead of bringing home $500 per month as a baseball player (slightly less than the average MLB salary these days), he devoted himself to full-time ministry at the YMCA for $83 each month. That is how America's most famous turn-of-the-century evangelist went from stealing bases in baseball stadiums to stealing souls from Satan in tabernacles across the country.

BLUFFING YOUR WAY THROUGH THEOLOGICAL DISCUSSIONS

Most Christians have never had the luxury of a seminary education, so you missed learning all those big words that can make you feel like you are in the theological know. You don't have to be left out in the cold. Imagine how impressed your friends will be when you casually throw out the word *perichoresis* in the next Sunday school class. Of course, they won't know whether it has any relevance whatsoever to the topic at hand, but just in case, here are some words and definitions that will allow you to bluff your way through just about any theological conversation.

Transubstantiation—This term refers to the Roman Catholic view that when the elements of the Mass are consecrated, the bread and wine actually become the physical body and blood of Jesus, even though they retain all the external physical characteristics of bread and wine.

Supralapsarianism—The Calvinist position that God decreed the election of those who would be saved as well as those who would experience damnation, and that he did so prior to (supra) decreeing the lapse (Fall) of Adam and Eve and, for that matter, prior to even creating the universe. This is a truly spiffy tool for the bluffer because it can be contrasted with sublapsarianism or infralapsarianism, which see the decrees of salvation and damnation as God's response to the decree that makes the Fall possible. Warning: this term should not be used in the presence of intense Calvinists (as if there is any other kind) since some of them actually know what it means.

Trichotomism—This view considers the human being to be a unity of three separate parts—body, soul and spirit. The soul is the part of the person that is thought to contain his or her individual personality, while the spirit is that which allows the person to enter into relationship with God.

Perichoresis—This term expresses the idea that any essential characteristic or action that can be attributed to one person of the Trinity should also be attributed to the other two persons. Thus, if God the Father is essentially infinite, this characteristic is true also for the Son and the Holy Spirit. This is actually an amazing three-for-the-price-of-one bluffer's special, because if anyone asks you what it means, you can simply say that it is synonymous with circumincession or coinherence.

Ubiquitarianism—The belief that, following his ascension, Christ is not just present throughout the universe in his divine nature, but in his human nature as well.

Adiaphora—Refers to theological matters that are not directly related to the question of salvation and/or are not explicitly mentioned or prohibited in Scripture.

Theodicy—This describes the attempt to address the question of how evil can exist if God is both good and all-powerful. Theodicy should not be confused with the sequel to Homer's *The Iliad*.

Exegesis—The process of drawing meaning out of the text of Scripture rather than imposing our biases on it (referred to as *eisegesis*). It expresses the ideal that we should let Scripture speak for itself. The fact that you see this word in print first is a fortunate thing. As a college freshman, Dr. Steve was told to purchase a book titled *New Testament Exegesis*, which he heard as *New Testament Acts of Jesus*. The smirk on the bookstore clerk's face when he asked for the latter title was enough to guarantee that he would never ask for directions or assistance again in his life. Dr. Steve suspects that most males have had such a defining moment.

PROLIFIC HYMNISTS

People today who would like to get rid of hymns should know how hard it was to get them into worship in the first place. The music in English churches in the late seventeenth century came exclusively from translations of the Psalms. This all changed when eighteen-year-old Isaac Watts grumbled to his father about how awful church music was, especially since the Psalms did not include the New Testament revelation. His dad, apparently unaware of the unwritten rule about challenging a teenage son, told him to try and do better.

As a result, young Isaac wrote a new hymn each week for the next 222 consecutive weekly services. Many of these were collected into a hymnal titled *Hymns and Spiritual Songs* (1707),

which included paraphrases of New Testament texts, something completely new in the English-speaking world. Innovations never come easy in the area of church music, and there was strong opposition to Watts's hymns from many quarters. Some churches even split over the issue (if you can imagine a church dividing over music).

Although controversial at first, Watts's idea of moving beyond the Psalms for the lyrics of hymns took off like wildfire. One famous hymnwriter, Charles Wesley, caught the fever in a big way. Over his life, he wrote at least 6,500 hymns. Charles, together with his brother, John, published sixty-four collections of hymns over a period of about fifty years. In fact, the first hymnal published in America was John Wesley's *Collection of Psalms and Hymns* (1737). Among Charles Wesley's best-known hymns are "Jesus, Lover of My Soul," "O for a Thousand Tongues," "Hark, the Herald Angels Sing" and "Christ the Lord Is Risen Today." In their spare time, the two Wesley brothers also founded the Methodist movement.

Despite Charles Wesley's prolific hymn writing, he comes in a distant second to Fanny Crosby, who penned over 9,000 of them. Among the most famous of these are "Blessed Assurance," "All the Way My Savior Leads Me" and "I Am Thine, O Lord." In addition to her hymnody, she taught at the New York Institute for the Blind for over twenty years; published several books and collections of poetry; worked extensively among the poor of the inner city; and memorized the first five books of the Old Testament, all the Gospels and much of the rest of the Bible. Impressed yet? We might also mention that she was blind from the age of six weeks. When she died at the age of ninety-five, her small headstone read "Aunt Fanny," followed by the first two lines from one of her most-loved hymns, "Blessed assurance, Jesus is mine! O what a foretaste of glory divine!"

Quite possibly the best-loved hymn in English is "Amazing Grace." Written by John Newton and appearing for the first time in a hymnal in 1779, the song was an autobiographical look back to a time when Newton was truly a wretch in need of some amazing grace. He had been the captain of a slave ship and had made several transatlantic passages bringing African slaves to the Americas. However, one night after a violent storm at sea, he took stock of his life and gave himself over to God. Later in life, Newton became a pastor and wrote hundreds of other hymns, though none would come close to the popularity of "Amazing Grace."

A current debate among musicologists is whether Newton would have written this hymn had he known that its words would fit perfectly with the music for the *Gilligan's Island* theme song. The growing consensus is that this was the plan all along. Think about it: Newton was a ship's captain; a ship's captain was stranded on Gilligan's Island. Newton "once was lost but now he's found"; Gilligan was once lost, and now he's found too, even if it did take a special two-hour episode a few years after the series was cancelled to reverse the results of their three-hour cruise.

If it bothers you too much to think of "Amazing Grace" sung to the theme of Gilligan's Island, it may comfort you to know that it also works with the tune of "Joy to the World" or "All Hail the Power of Jesus' Name."

THE SERENITY PRAYER

Once you get past the Lord's Prayer, "Now I lay me down to sleep . . ." and "Rub-a-Dub-Dub, thanks for the grub," perhaps the best-known prayer to American Christians is the so-called Serenity Prayer. For those not familiar with it, the Serenity Prayer, in its most popular form, goes,

God, grant me the SERENITY to accept the things
I cannot change;
COURAGE to change the things I can;
and the WISDOM to know the difference.

This prayer, actually a portion of a longer prayer, was written by Reinhold Niebuhr, a theologian at Union Theological Seminary in New York. A couple years later, in 1934, it appeared in a book that was a compilation of prayers.

☞ SERENITY AND AA

The prayer's popularity got a huge boost when it came to the attention of Bill W., cofounder of Alcoholics Anonymous. Bill W. read the prayer to the AA staff, and they thought it fit the purposes of their organization so well that they had thousands of cards printed with the Serenity Prayer on it. A few years later during World War II, the prayer was once again printed on wallet-sized cards and handed out to soldiers by the USO. To this day the Serenity Prayer is seen as a prominent cornerstone of the AA philosophy, appearing in much of their official literature and repeated at most meetings. It has also been picked up for use by many of the 12-Step groups that have grown out of the original Alcoholics Anonymous organization.

As we see below, the longer version of the Serenity Prayer also supplies the "One day at a time" slogan so closely associated with AA. The full version of the prayer ends with these words:

Living ONE DAY AT A TIME;
enjoying one moment at a time;
accepting hardships as the pathway to peace;

Taking, as He did, this sinful world
as it is, not as I would have it;

Trusting that He will make all things
right if I surrender to His Will;
that I may be reasonably happy in this life
and supremely happy with Him forever in the next. Amen.

☞ VARIATIONS FOR THOSE NOT INTO SERENITY

For those who are slightly more cynical, don't despair. There may be a variation more to your liking. For curmudgeons, there is the "Anti-Serenity Prayer," which reads:

> God grant me the anxiety to try to control the things I cannot control,
> the fear to avoid the things I can,
> and the neurosis to deny the difference.

Although a bit more difficult to remember, you also have the "Senility Prayer":

> God, grant me the senility to forget the people I never liked anyway,
> the good fortune to run into the ones that I do,
> and the eyesight to tell the difference.

FROM SAINT TO SANTA

Most of us are well enough acquainted with Santa Claus to know that he often goes by the alias of St. Nick. But who is this St. Nick guy, and how did he morph into the jolly, chubby guy with a red suit?

St. Nick is actually Saint Nicholas (or Nicholas of Myra to be exact, since there are twenty-one saints named Nicholas, plus one Saint Nichole, who should not be confused with Mrs. Santa). The Saint Nicholas of history did not live anywhere close to the North

Pole, but resided in Asia Minor—modern-day Turkey—in the fourth century.

DOWRIES, IN THE NICK OF TIME

He was reputed to have been the son of well-to-do and pious parents who died during an epidemic while Nicholas was young. Nicholas was determined to use his inheritance in a charitable way, which brings us to the best-known story about him. A certain nobleman had fallen on hard times and could not afford dowries for his three daughters. As a result, he was fearful that they would have to be sold into prostitution. In one version of the story, Nicholas is moved by their plight to toss a small bag of gold into the window of the nobleman's house, where it landed in a stocking drying near the fireplace. Here we have, then, the origin of putting gifts in stockings placed on the fireplace mantle (and Dr. Steve would have to say that gold in the stocking beats the dickens out of the "soap-on-a-rope" he got in his stocking one Christmas). Chucking the gold down the chimney is a version that came along centuries later.

In any case, the gold provided the dowry for the oldest daughter, who was promptly married off to a suitable suitor. As the other two daughters grew up, Nicholas repeated his throw-the-bag-of-gold-through-the-window routine for their dowries as well. However, while making his delivery for the youngest daughter, the nobleman caught Nicholas in the act. Ignoring Nick's desire to remain anonymous, he spread the story of the future saint's generosity.

FROM BISHOP TO SAINT

Years later, Nicholas was elevated to the office of bishop in the provincial city of Myra even though he was a layperson (a practice not unheard of during that time), based on his reputation for piety and charity. The timing of this promotion was rather unfortunate, because a nasty persecution of Christians by the Emperor Diocletian was underway. The new bishop was almost immediately arrested, imprisoned and tortured for several years before gaining his freedom under Constantine. He governed as bishop in Myra for almost three decades and is thought to have died in 346 on December 6, which later became the feast day commemorating him.

Although no one knows when Nicholas was canonized, he quickly became a very popular saint. A basilica honoring him was constructed in Constantinople in 430, and it is believed that his image appeared on more Byzantine seals during the Middle Ages than that of any saint except for Mary. Four

hundred English churches were dedicated to him during the same period. Because of the story above, combined with reports of other acts of mercy toward children (including one in which his fervent prayers brought back to life three young boys who had been hacked to death by an evil butcher and placed in a barrel of brine), he became the patron saint of children and unmarried maidens.

🐿 HOW THE DUTCH CREATED SANTA

The next major phase in the transition from Saint Nicholas to Santa Claus requires a fast-forward of several centuries to New York City. Saint Nicholas (or Sint Nikolaas, frequently contracted to Sinter Klaas in Dutch) had been a favorite of the Dutch for centuries. Even the negative view of saints that came with the Dutch Reformation did little to snuff out Christmas traditions in Holland, which included leaving treats in shoes on Christmas Eve. These traditions traveled to America when the Dutch founded New Amsterdam and endured even after the Brits took over and renamed the place New York.

To help retain the memory of New York's Dutch heritage, Saint Nicholas was proclaimed the patron saint of the city in 1804. Five years later, Washington Irving published a short fiction piece to commemorate Saint Nicholas Day, which featured a rotund Saint Nicholas with a clay pipe. The story claimed that the first emigrant ship to reach the new colony had a Saint Nicholas figurehead and that the first church in the city was dedicated to him, neither of which is true. The part of this piece that caught on like wildfire, however, was the idea that the saint shimmied down chimneys with gifts for the children.

Gas was poured on the fire in 1823 with a poem now known as "The Night Before Christmas," which gave Sinter Klaas, now Santa Claus, his furry outfit, the "bundle of toys . . . flung on his back," a snowy beard and the belly that shook "like a bowlful of jelly" when he laughed. (Just for the record, medieval images of Saint Nicholas included a beard, but his middle region was a lot leaner.) Over the years, the visual image of Santa Claus was modified and shaped by annual drawings in *Harper's Weekly* and Coca-Cola advertisements until he assumed the rather standard Santa look we all know today.

There you have the sketchy outline of the shift from Saint to Santa, from Asia Minor to North Pole, from young-Elvis skinny to old-Elvis fat, from charity to commercialization. I think I like the old "Santa" better.

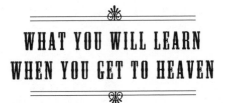

WHAT YOU WILL LEARN
WHEN YOU GET TO HEAVEN

How often have you heard someone, faced with life's great imponderables, exclaim that we'll just have to wait until we get to heaven so we can ask God? While we are still waiting for the answers, it might be a good idea to know what the questions are. To this end, we have compiled the official top ten list of questions people want to ask God.

10. So where did the other sock go?

9. Did it ever get old hearing, "They Will Know We Are Christians by Our Love?"

8. Did anyone ever finish singing "One Thousand Bottles of Beer on the Wall?"

7. The accordion wasn't your idea, was it?

6. What percentage of the time were people right when they said, "It's a God thing?"

5. Did you doze off for a while during the '70s? If not, how do we make sense of disco?

4. Would split pea soup have been more popular if it were a different color?

3. Would it be possible for you to create a world in which male pattern baldness is considered a major turn-on by female members of the species?

2. I don't suppose you ever lose at Rock, Paper, Scissors, do you?

1. What about that "Can God make a rock so big he couldn't lift it" question? Ever do that just for the heck of it?

WWJD?

Perhaps no acronym is more familiar to American Christianity than WWJD, or "What Would Jesus Do?" The current popularity of this almost omnipresent set of letters has been traced to a youth leader in Holland, Michigan, Janie Tinklenberg, back in 1989. Tinklenberg wanted something concrete to remind her youth group about their commitment to follow Christ. A book she had often read gave her an idea, so Tinklenberg got in touch with Lesco Corporation, which manufactures promotional products. They made a batch of bracelets with WWJD printed on them, and the idea took off. It is estimated that since that first batch of a few hundred bracelets, more than fifteen million have been sold, not to mention all the WWJD backpacks, baseball caps, coffee mugs, key chains and other products that have followed.

THE BOOK BEHIND WWJD

What book is the inspiration behind all the WWJD paraphernalia? It is actually one of the most widely read books of the twentieth century, although fewer people today are aware of it than the products it inspired. The book behind the bracelet is a simple little novel titled *In His Steps*, written by a Congregationalist pastor named Charles M. Sheldon.

In 1889, Sheldon had taken the pastorate of the recently established Central Congregational Church in Topeka, Kansas. Under him, the church grew quickly to three morning services and a Sunday evening worship. At first, the evening service was poorly attended, so Sheldon came up with a unique plan to increase the numbers. He had been a writer since his youth, and he began to produce what he called "sermon stories." Sheldon would read a chapter of these sermon stories each week during the evening service. Each week's chapter ended at a critical moment in the story, and people looked forward to the resolution of the cliffhanger the next week. Soon, the evening service was full. *In His Steps* was one of the books written for the "sermon stories."

The *In His Steps* sermon series was especially popular with Sheldon's congregation, and it was quickly picked up by the *Chicago Advance* newspaper, which published it as a serial, one chapter each week. It proved to be extremely popular with the *Advance's* readers, so the next year, 1897, they brought it out as a book. However, the *Advance* messed up on getting the book properly copyrighted, and it went immediately into public domain. As a result, several companies published it, and since they did not have to pay royalties, Sheldon received almost nothing for a book that by some estimates has been translated into almost fifty languages and has sold over thirty million copies. Sheldon, in a forward to a later edition of the book, says, "I do not need to say that I am very thankful that owing to the defective copyright the book has had a larger reading on account of the great number of publishers." There are several publishers today who keep the book in print, and it is also available online from several websites.

☞ *IN HIS STEPS*—THE STORY LINE

In His Steps is set in the fictional city of Raymond (which resembles in many respects the actual city of Topeka at the end of the nineteenth century, which, in turn, resembles the actual city of Topeka at the beginning of the twenty-first century). As the book opens, an out-of-work printer arrives on a Friday at the office of Rev. Henry Maxwell, asking for help. Maxwell, who is busy preparing his sermon, is not certain how to help the homeless man and sends him on his way.

On Sunday the same man appears at First Church, rises after the sermon, walks down the middle aisle and begins to speak of his plight. He had lost his job ten months earlier, his wife had died four months before, and his little girl was staying with another family until he found work. He then says,

> I heard some people singing at a church prayer meeting the other night,
>
> All for Jesus, all for Jesus,
> All my being's ransomed powers
> All my thoughts, and all my doings,
> All my days, and all my hours,
>
> And I kept wondering as I sat on the steps outside just what they meant by it. It seems to me there's an awful lot of trouble in the world that somehow wouldn't exist if all the people who sing such songs went and lived them out. I suppose I don't understand. But what would Jesus do? Is that what you mean by following His steps?

The man then collapsed, and died a week later.

In the next Sunday's sermon, Rev. Maxwell has a challenge for his congregation. He asks for volunteers who will vow to ask themselves the same question over the next year that the unemployed printer had asked them all the previous Sunday—"What would Jesus do?" The rest of the book follows the stories of those who took up the challenge, and those who did not.

☛ WHAT WOULD SHELDON DO?

In His Steps reflects the concerns that Rev. Sheldon brought to his ministry. When he arrived in Topeka, he found a city deep in economic depression. To better understand the situation facing the down-and-out, the young minister dressed in shabby clothes and went out for a week, seeking a job. Throughout his career, he continued to go into various parts of the community to gain an insider's look at everyday life. He would clerk in stores, ride the trains with the brakemen and follow doctors on their rounds. Later in his life he was given the chance by the publisher of the Topeka daily paper to be editor in chief for a week, running things by asking "What would Jesus do?"

Sheldon was also a key figure in a new movement at that time—the kindergarten. He and members of his church started two kindergartens. One was in the middle of Topeka at Central Congregational; the other was in Tennesseetown, an extremely poor black community near Topeka populated by emancipated slaves and their children. The latter was the first black kindergarten in the western United States. One graduate of this kindergarten program became Topeka's first black lawyer, whose own son, Charles Sheldon Scott (so named in appreciation to Sheldon), became the lawyer who argued and won the landmark desegregation case—*Brown v. Topeka Board of Education*—before the Supreme Court.

One interesting little bit of irony emerges when we look at Sheldon in the context of the WWJD trend that he inspired with his book. Many of the evangelically oriented people who sport a wardrobe full of WWJD clothing use words like "liberal" and "social gospel" to describe all that can go wrong with Christianity. However, Sheldon, with his theological perspective and deep concern about the material and educational needs of people, placed himself squarely in the social gospel tradition of his day.

Over his long life, Sheldon wrote about fifty books and hundreds of articles and newspaper columns. Nothing else he penned, however, came anywhere close to the popularity of *In His Steps.* This book, criticized in its day as idealistic and simplistic, has challenged Christians for over one hundred years to think about their actions through the straightforward and searching question, "What would Jesus do?"

THE VULGAR BIBLE

You are aware, I'm sure, that the Bible has been translated into a large number of languages. Did you know, though, that a *vulgar* translation exists? Sound like some quirky version created by a twisted person with too much time to kill? Actually, the translator was one of the greatest minds in history, and his vulgar Bible was the standard translation of Scripture for the largest branch of the Christian church for almost 1,500 years. No kidding.

A LANGUAGE EVERYONE UNDERSTANDS

For the earliest Christians, the Greek of the New Testament presented little obstacle since almost everyone had some proficiency in that language. Moreover, the Greek translation of the Old Testament (the Septuagint, usually abbreviated LXX) had been around for a couple of centuries before Christianity, so it was accessible to the early Christians as well. However, what do you do when knowledge of Greek begins to disappear in many increasingly Christianized parts of the world? The obvious decision is to start translating, and the obvious choice for the language was Latin, quite popular at the time, courtesy of the Roman Empire. In fact, Latin translations began to appear around A.D. 200. The problem here was that these translations were prepared by any Tom, Dick or Herodius who happened to have a hankering to do some translating. As a result, no standard Latin translation existed, and those in existence often were just not very good.

In A.D. 383, Pope Damasus I decided to commission a Latin translation that would unite the church (which, ironically, had the opposite effect on the Greek-speaking eastern branch of the Christian church, further driving a wedge between it and the western church). He called upon the highly learned Jerome to undertake the task. Jerome got started right away with a translation of the Gospels from the Greek, which he completed in 384. From there, he went to work on the Old Testament, first working mostly from the Septuagint, but later relying primarily on the Masoretic text in Hebrew (with some help from several rabbis). He got into some tricky political ground in the Psalms, since many Western churches had used the Old Latin translation in worship for decades. To accommodate sensibilities, he eventually produced three versions of the Psalms: one that only slightly revised the familiar language of the Old Latin, a second that used the Hebrew text to correct the Old Latin and a third that was a completely new translation from the Masoretic text.

☞ WHY WAS JEROME'S TRANSLATION VULGAR?

In all, Jerome spread his work out over a twenty-year period. The result is what is now referred to as the Vulgate Bible. "Vulgate" comes from the Latin word *vulgaris*, which is, indeed, the origin of our English word *vulgar*. However, it had a slightly different connotation back in old Jerome's day. Instead of "nasty," *vulgar* meant "ordinary" or "common." It is often thought that the Vulgate was so called because it was written in the common Latin of the marketplace rather than the more literary Latin of the classical poets and orators. While it is true that Jerome's translation does use the more vernacular form of Latin, we must look elsewhere for its designation as Vulgate.

Jerome himself spoke of a *vulgata editio* of Scripture, but he was not talking about his own translation. He uses *vulgata* instead to refer to the Septuagint, a designation that translation maintained throughout the Middle Ages. Jerome's translation, in contrast, was usually called the *editio nostra*, or new edition (not to be confused with Kenny Rogers's old band, The First Edition). It only formally acquired the label "Vulgate" at the Council of Trent, the council that met in response to the growth of Protestantism.

With the proliferation of Protestant translations of Scripture, Roman Catholics decided they needed to bolster support for their traditional version. In 1546 the Council of Trent put its official seal of approval on Jerome's *editio nostra* as the *vetus et vulgata editio* (ancient and common edition). Thus, with the stroke of a pen, Jerome's version went from being "new" to "ancient." More importantly, it was now designated as the common *(vulgata)* Bible of the Catholic church ("common," as in the only one officially permitted for use in the church).

One small problem with this "common" Bible was that no one was really sure which version of the Vulgate was the common one. After centuries of hand-copying, quite a number of mistakes and corruptions had crept into the text, so variants were found in different versions of the Vulgate. In 1592 an official version of the Vulgate that eliminated all the variants was prepared under the order of Pope Clement VIII. Known as the Clementine Vulgate, this edition remained the standard and was unchanged until updated again in 1907.

There you have it. *Vulgar*, which now means "naughty and

nasty," once meant "ordinary and common," although at times today it does seem that nasty is far too common. If nothing else, the shifting definitions taken on by words remind us of one reason Bible translation is an ongoing process.

"HEY SIMEON, CAN YOU SEE MY HOUSE FROM UP THERE?"

The stories of those who take faith seriously enough to endure hardships for it are generally inspiring to hear. Can this be taken too far? We'll let you be the judge of whether spiritual athleticism got a bit out of hand with Simeon the Elder.

Growing up, Simeon was an illiterate shepherd boy who determined that he had been called to be a monk. To prepare for this vocation, he spent a summer buried up to his neck. Once ready to seek admittance, he fell on the ground outside the monastery gates and lay there for five full days. The monks let Simeon in, but his stay there was to be short.

The usual rigors of monastic life weren't quite stringent enough, so Simeon tied ropes so tightly around his body that the flesh grew over them, limited himself to one meal a week and walled himself in during Lent so he would not be tempted to eat. The abbot decided that Simeon had gone a bit overboard, so the young monk, expelled after a year, headed for the desert mountains of Syria.

📖 MOVING ON UP

Simeon spent the first few years of his desert existence living in a cave or on a narrow ledge, but as stories of his holiness and healing power increased, he found that the solitude he desired was quickly disappearing. People kept coming to the desert in increasing numbers to seek advice or healing, and some went so far as attempting to tear patches from his robe to use as holy relics. Instead of moving out, Simeon moved up—to a small platform atop a nine-foot pillar. Once he moved up to the top of the pillar, he stayed up: thirty-seven years to be exact. No shelter from the searing desert heat or the rain and snow of winter. In fact, he kept moving up, the height of the pillar eventually reaching almost sixty feet during the last thirty years of his stay.

What do you do on top of a pillar for almost four decades? Simeon spent most of his time praying, arms outstretched toward the sky. He became one of the most popular tourist stops in the Syrian desert and would preach twice a day to those assembled at the base of the pillar. He also occasionally dictated letters to be sent to church officials and even emperors. And he bowed a lot. One observer counted 1,244 repetitions of bowing during his prayers before he gave up the count. One thing Simeon did not do much of was eating, limiting himself to one meal per week.

At the age of about seventy, Simeon died. He had become so popular that his body had to be put under guard in Antioch out of fear that neighboring towns would seek to procure all or parts of his body. However, it was reported about a hundred years later that some of the teeth had been removed from his skull as relics. Simeon's example inspired a whole new generation of monks, known as the Stylites (from *stylos* = pillar), who also lived on columns. One such follower, Alipius, stood on a pillar, without sitting, for fifty-three years until he lost the use of his legs, after which he had to lie atop the pillar for the last fourteen years of his life.

THE AMISH

You probably know about Pennsylvania's famous "Amish Country" in Lancaster County, but what do you know about the Amish who live there? It might be helpful to start with the fact that Amish are not isolated to the state of Pennsylvania. The largest concentration of Amish folk is actually in Ohio, but they also reside in more than twenty states in the U.S., as well as in Ontario, Canada. There are approximately 150,000 Amish.

THE AMISH MIGRATION

Although the Amish now live exclusively in North America, they did not get their start here. Their roots are in the Anabaptist movement that grew out of post-Reformation Europe. The Amish split from the Mennonites in 1693 and were led by Jacob Amman, from whom they get their name. Because they were often subject to persecution in their European homelands for their religious beliefs and refusal to serve in the military (the Amish were, and are, pacifists), they began to seek a place where they could worship and live freely.

William Penn founded the colony of Pennsylvania with the then-unique idea of religious tolerance. This resulted in an early wave of Amish immigration to Pennsylvania in the years between 1730 and 1770. A second large group came to America between 1820 and 1860, primarily settling in states other than Pennsylvania, since religious toleration had since become the law of the land. Eventually, the Amish ceased to exist in Europe, due to emigration and assimilation.

☛ THE AMISH AND "THE ENGLISH"

While most of their beliefs are quite consistent with those of other Christians, one idea that gives the Amish their distinctive character is their belief in strict separation from the world. As a result, they live and worship apart from outsiders, referred to as "the English." Their refusal to wire homes for electricity comes from a reluctance to be connected to the outside world—they often have energy sources for farm use that are not linked to external power grids.

Separation from the outside world is also evident in Amish dress, their use of buggies instead of cars, and the fact that they retain use of the Pennsylvania Dutch dialect for everyday conversation and German in worship. The Amish also learn English in their schools, which are Amish run and go only through eighth grade. An-

other way separation is practiced is in *Streng Meidung*, or shunning. When a member becomes too worldly or leaves the group, the family is prohibited from social interaction with the errant individual, with the goal that he or she will return to the community.

☛ THE REAL "SIMPLE LIFE"

Another distinctive quality of Amish life is simplicity and humility. Their rejection of most modern technologies is not due to a refusal to change, but out of concern that technology may interfere with their lifestyle of simplicity and family cohesiveness. All women wear solid-colored dresses, and all males wear dark suits (made at home), so even their simple clothing reflects their religious conviction that showy dress leads to pride, and thus interferes with equality. Ironically, then, the style of dress intended to make them blend in with each other causes them to stand out when they venture beyond their communities.

The difficulty of maintaining simplicity throughout a lifetime, something outsiders are quick to note, is a factor that the Amish themselves are aware of. Thus, many Amish groups have a tradition known as *rumspringa*, which literally means "running around." Since baptism marks their full entry into the Amish community and does not occur until just prior to marriage, teens are not held to the same standards as full-fledged members. Thus, those sixteen through about twenty, while still living at home, are allowed a significant amount of freedom to date, interact with outsiders, wear non-Amish clothing and even engage in a few very un-Amish vices such as drinking. Presumably, buggy races with dad's "wheels" are a part of this ritual. The purpose of *rumspringa* is to allow a person to enter baptism with full knowledge of the options. In the end, only about 10 to 15 percent of Amish teens decide to leave the community.

DID YOU KNOW?
Who's In, Who's Out at Westminster Abbey

Although considered by many one of the chief enemies of the church, Charles Darwin is buried in one. His mortal remains are buried in Westminster Abbey, alongside some of England's most prominent citizens. Another famous Brit, Oliver Cromwell, was also buried in Westminster Abbey, but was removed from his crypt two years later and posthumously "executed." While his body was thrown into an unmarked pit, his severed head did get to stay close to Westminster Abbey for a while: it was displayed outside the church doors for four years—at the end of a spike.

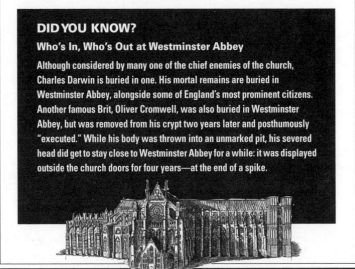

ONE OF HISTORY'S MOST SIGNIFICANT DIETS

One of the more famous diets of history is the Diet of Worms. No, it isn't one of those faddish weight-loss plans, although it sounds like it might be effective (night crawlers are chock full of protein, with almost no fat). The "Worms" in the Diet of Worms is actually a town in Germany, and the German pronunciation makes Worms a bit more palatable. You turn the *W* into a *V* sound, you make the *o* long, and you spit at least twice to get the proper German inflection. The "Diet" in the Diet of Worms refers to the official gathering that met in 1521 to give Martin Luther one last chance to recant his ideas.

At the Diet, when pressed on his ideas for reforming the church, Luther said, "Unless I am convinced by the testimony of the Scriptures or by clear reason, I am bound by the Scriptures I have quoted and my conscience is captive to the Word of God. I cannot and I will not retract anything, since it is neither safe nor right to go against conscience."

Nothing is recorded about whether anyone lost any weight with this Diet, but Luther probably would have lost his life had he not come under the protection of his Prince Frederick the Wise of Saxony. With the Diet of Worms, however, the Protestant Reformation began and the Roman Catholic Church lost its monopoly on Western Christianity.

HOAXES AND URBAN MYTHS

If you have e-mail, you have almost certainly received a few. I'm talking about urban legends and e-mail hoaxes. These myths have always been around. In the past, they spread through chain letters, radio and print. Today, the speed with which they spread over the Internet has only made the problem worse. The amazing thing is that, once out there, these stories take on a life of their own, and there is almost no way to kill them. The hoaxes are attached to every facet of life, but the Christian world has extended the life span of its share of mythical stories. Sometimes they are just silly. However, the perpetuation of some of these legends shows a sad tendency to believe the worst and an irresponsibility in checking out even the most basic facts. Below are some of the most common hoaxes circulating in religious broadcasting, church bulletins and e-mail chains.

☛ MADALYN MURRAY O'HAIR AND FCC PETITION #RM2493

One urban legend has been circulating through Christian circles since 1974, and has to be considered a classic. Madalyn Murray O'Hair was the head of American Atheists for years, which made her a target of many Christians. In addition, she had an extremely acerbic personality, so she really got under the skin of some people. In the mid-1970s, a rumor began that she had started a petition to have all religious broadcasters banned from the airwaves.

The minor problem is that she never circulated any such petition, although it would not have broken her heart if such programming had been eliminated.

The small element of fact in this (and it is very small) is that two men did petition the Federal Communications Commission in 1974 to freeze new applications from religious groups for use of channels and FM frequencies *reserved for educational purposes.* That petition was turned down *in 1975.* That should have been the end of it, right? Well, the whole thing keeps popping up, and literally millions of letters have been sent to the FCC and various public officials, protesting this petition, and they are still arriving today.

One really odd thing about the continued connection between O'Hair and this particular rumor is that she disappeared in 1995. It was determined that she had been murdered at that time when her body was found in 2000.

☞ PROCTER, GAMBLE AND SATAN

Another classic hoax began as a chain letter about twenty years ago. The story is that Procter and Gamble's president appeared on a number of TV talk shows and proclaimed himself a disciple of Satan. The man-in-the-moon logo of the company was also supposed to have satanic symbolism. This led to calls for a boycott of all the company's products, which is really quite a list (no Pampers for Junior anymore), because company profits funded satanic organizations.

There are just a few minor problems with this whole thing. First, no president or any other executive of the company has been on any of the talk shows listed in any version of the chain letters and e-mail missives. Second, the man-in-the-moon logo has been the company's symbol since 1851, so you now have to assume P&G has been a satanic front group for over 150 years. Finally, since Procter and Gamble is a publicly traded company, they are required to disclose what they do with their money. No satanic groups made the donor list.

A REAL HELL HOLE

A hot story has found its way into the rumor mill, thanks mostly to some high visibility given to it by the Trinity Broadcasting Network (TBN). The legend is that geologists had drilled a well in remote Siberia that reached almost ten miles down when the drill bit stopped biting. These scientists determined that they had reached the hollow center of our fine planet, and lowered microphones through the hole. As they listened in, they heard the anguished screams and moans of the multitudes suffering in hell. The temperature of Hades was measured at 2,000 degrees.

There was, in fact, a well drilled in that region to about the depth reported, but the temperature was about 1,820 degrees less than the hoax reported (though at 180 degrees, still warm enough to make Death Valley in August seem downright chilly). Also, they did not find a hollow center, except in a chocolate Easter bunny they pulled out of the hole (okay, I made up that last part, but who knows, you might get an e-mail about it some day), and no screaming was audible. No one quite knows how a story about a deep hole in the middle of nowhere morphed into an account of a deep hole into the middle of hell, but it's out there.

DR. PEPPER IS AN ATHEIST

An e-mail rumor circulated on several Christian websites and in church bulletin announcements that Dr. Pepper was releasing a can that had printed on it the Pledge of Allegiance without the words "under God" included. Of course, it was accompanied by calls to boycott the company's products and to write Dr. Pepper and express deep displeasure. This controversy, most likely intensified by a court decision about the same time that questioned the constitutionality of "under God" in the pledge, was based on a very thin sliver of truth.

The reality is that Dr. Pepper did print a can in a limited geographical area that contained three words from the Pledge of Allegiance—"One Nation, Indivisible." So it is a fact that the words "under God" were excluded, but the remaining twenty-six words in the pledge were nowhere in sight either.

☞ NASA FINDS A MISSING DAY

This is one case where the source of the myth can be discovered. The president of Curtis Engine Company, Harold Hill, claimed to be a consultant to NASA when he witnessed this event, and recorded it in a book titled *How to Live Like a King's Kid.* Hill states that scientists at NASA were running a computer program to ensure that they would not send a satellite into a trajectory that would put it on a collision course with the planets, moon, sun and the other stuff that floats around up there. As the computers went through their calculations, they ground to a halt, leaving these great scientists flummoxed. Then a Christian on the team remembered hearing about a story in which the sun stood still for a day. They dug out a Bible and looked up Joshua 10:12-13, which says that "the sun stood still, and the moon stopped . . . and did not hurry to set for about a whole day."

The scientists fed this new information into the computer and it started happily whirring away for a while, but then stopped again. The Christian scientist then remembered another story about the sun going backwards, and so they went to 2 Kings 20:11: "The prophet Isaiah cried to the LORD; and he brought the shadow back the ten intervals, by which the sun had declined on the dial of Ahaz." The scientists did some calculations, and determined that this amount of reverse solar movement would amount to a forty-minute period. This new data was put in, and whammo! the program worked like a charm. NASA had confirmed what the Bible said about these two missing time periods, which added up to a perfect twenty-four hours.

A lot of things turn out to be downright fishy about this whole story. First, Mr. Hill was not a consultant to NASA in any technical sense, although his company did have a contract to service some of NASA's electrical generators. He later admitted that he did not witness any of the alleged events, but still maintained that he had heard them secondhand. A second problem is that there is no way to calculate whether a day is missing without some fixed reference that would have occurred prior to the missing twenty-four hours supposedly found by NASA. A third problem is that one does not have to go back this far to calculate the orbits of the celestial bodies to ensure the safety of whatever we might blast up there. Finally, the whole story hinges on the phrase in Joshua 10:13 that states that the sun stood still for "about a whole day." How the scientists came to determine that "about a day" equals exactly twenty-three hours and twenty minutes is a mystery, but this would have had to be their conclusion in order to make room for the extra forty minutes they would have to later add to account for the passage in 2 Kings. But all this is necessary to get a clean and tidy twenty-four-hour day. Perhaps the only fact we can really know from this clock-adjustment story is that Mr. Hill had too much time on his hands.

☞ I'M NOT GOING TO BE LEFT BEHIND

My personal choice for the gullibility award concerns a recent hoax about a woman who crawled out the sunroof of a moving car and jumped to her death, believing that the rapture was underway (no word on who would get to keep the car had she been correct).

She was reportedly convinced of the rapture's occurrence because she saw people floating heavenward and a robed man, supposed to be Jesus, at the side of the road with his arms raised.

According to the story, which carried a bogus Associated Press reference, this unfortunate incident was set off by an odd chain of events. A man who resembled Jesus was heading to a toga party in his pickup. A tarp covering the bed of the truck came loose, which caused the twelve helium-filled, life-sized sex dolls inside to begin floating away. When the driver got the pickup stopped, all he could do was raise his hands in frustration as he watched his party props disappear into the sky. By the way, this story, albeit with a different location and different names than the original, was picked up and printed by the always reliable *Weekly World News.*

The source of the story? It was written by Elroy Willis on an Internet site called *Religion in the News.* Apparently, someone did not notice the warning on the site that says, "Some of the stories are really true. See if you can figure out which ones they are." This one wasn't.

Just a bit of advice—before hitting the "forward" button and encouraging the idea that all Christians are gullible idiots, take a look at one of the many sites that catalog hoaxes. Snopes.com and truthminers.com are generally good at keeping track of bogus stories.

DID YOU KNOW?

Martyrs Must Be Properly Attired

One of the earliest theologians of Christianity was Origen, who died about 250. He almost didn't live long enough to achieve this fame, however. When he was about seventeen, a fierce persecution broke out and Origen's father, Leonides, was arrested and sentenced to death for his faith. Origen was determined to go and receive martyrdom with his father but was prevented from doing so when his mother hid his clothes from him.

YOIDO

In 1958 a new church was started by two Assemblies of God pastors in South Korea. Despite publicizing the first worship service throughout the neighborhood, the congregation's initial meeting was attended by the three daughters of one of the pastors, and an elderly woman looking to get out of the rain. It wasn't a great beginning, and a further complicating factor was that one of the pastors was soon to become the mother-in-law of the other. In twenty years, however, this fledgling congregation would grow to be the largest church in the world.

THE EARLY YEARS

The two intrepid pastors, Yonggi Cho and Choi Ja-shil, persisted by aggressively knocking on doors and providing help to their neighbors. Within the first year, the church had reached fifty members and outgrew Choi Ja-shil's living room. They moved to a tent in the backyard and continued to burst out of tents of increasing size. By 1961, they had one thousand members, and purchased their first piece of land in Soedaemun.

Just when things looked like they were really on a roll, Yonggi Cho was called up for his required military service. However, he was stationed at a base near Seoul and was able to continue preaching on Sundays. A short time after induction, he had a serious illness that led to his discharge from military duties. By 1968, the church had grown to eight thousand, and Cho was working himself to exhaustion.

Knowing that something had to change, he divided Seoul into zones and assigned members to cells, small groups that met in members' homes midweek. Men were reluctant to lead these groups, so the majority of cell leaders were (and still are) women, a move that did not seem to fit the patriarchal nature of Korean society. Nevertheless, the original 125 cell groups were wildly successful and brought about even more rapid growth.

THE YOIDO YEARS

By 1970, the Soedaemun location was completely inadequate, and the absence of large spaces in crowded Seoul created a crisis for the church. They made a bold move by purchasing Yoido Island, an unoccupied patch of land in the middle of the Han River with no bridge to provide access. Shortly after construction on the new church began, a severe economic downturn put the entire project in jeopardy. They persisted, and the new facility, named the Yoido Full Gospel Church, was opened in 1973. By 1977, the membership was 100,000; four years later it had doubled again.

In 1983 the auditorium size was expanded to seat 25,000, but even with seven services offered each Sunday, the church could not handle all the people. Cho began to plant satellite congregations, and even as some original parishioners migrated to the outlying congregations, new members continued to fill the Yoido church. Current membership is reported to be 800,000. If Yoido Full Gospel Church was a U.S. city, it would be the twelfth largest in the country, just between Detroit and Indianapolis.

YOIDO TODAY

How do you keep a church with 800,000 going? First, services run all day on Sunday in the main auditorium, with starting times all the way from 7:00 a.m. to 7:30 p.m. Cho's sermons are also sent to satellite churches via video feed. All sermons are in Korean, but if you attend, simultaneous translation is provided in Chinese, Russian, French, English and a number of other languages. Cho also gets a bit of help. Yoido has over 500 pastors (half female) and about 90,000 deacons (about 75 percent female).

Any church that gets to be this size is obviously going to be a target of criticism. Cho, who changed his name to Paul Yonggi Cho in the 1970s and more recently to David Yonggi Cho (he appears unreceptive to the efforts of some U.S. followers to change his name again to Jabez Yonggi Cho), has been charged with interjecting shamanism and occult views into his teaching, usually by individuals who level similar charges at their own mothers. Others are annoyed about his Pentecostal theology or his expansive use of women in leadership roles.

More recently, some outsiders were rankled when Cho changed his decision to step down at the age of seventy, as denominational rules require. Cho used a loophole that allows retirement to be postponed until age seventy-five if the church agrees. Not surprisingly, the church voted overwhelmingly to keep him in charge. That keeps him in the pulpit until 2010 or until Yoido Full Gospel Church catches up with Dallas, Texas, (1,200,000) in size, whichever comes first.

DID YOU KNOW?
Anonymous Angels

Angels are frequently mentioned in Scripture, but are rarely mentioned by name. The only angels named in the Bible are Michael, Gabriel and Lucifer.

SMALL POTATOES IN A MEGACHURCH WORLD

With about one thousand American churches now at the unofficial "megachurch" benchmark of two thousand attendees per week, you might think that the U.S. is the big fish in the megachurch pond. The reality, however, is very different. The biggest of the U.S. megachurches, Lakewood Church in Houston, Texas (average weekly attendance of about 25,000), does not even crack the top twenty worldwide.

That's right. The twenty largest churches by weekly participation are outside the U.S.A. The biggest in the world, Yoido Full Gospel Church in Seoul, South Korea, dwarfs Lakeland Church about ten to one, with an attendance of over 250,000 per week at its Yoido campus and satellite congregations. Other super-churches are found in places such as India, Argentina and Côte d'Ivoire. In fact, about half of the twenty largest churches are in the Southern Hemisphere, where the growth of Christianity is far outstripping that of the Northern Hemisphere.

DID YOU KNOW?

One Big Audience

Popes can draw a crowd, but the biggest one on record is when Pope John Paul II visited the Philippines in 1995 and said Mass to a crowd estimated at five million.

FAMILIAR PHRASES FROM KING JAMES

Most people never really realize how many of the familiar phrases, proverbs and clichés that form so much of our conversation have come to us from the King James Version of the Bible. Think you can spot them? The quiz below will "separate the sheep from the goats" (see Matthew 25:32) and determine who gets to "divide the plunder" (see Isaiah 9:3).

Circle the phrases you think are from the Bible and check pages 160-61 for your answers.

1. Drop in the bucket

2. Needle in a haystack

3. Out of the mouths of babes

4. How do you like them apples?

5. When hell freezes over

6. One swallow does not a summer make.

7. A fly in the ointment

8. Give me liberty or give me death.

9. Set your teeth on edge

10. By the skin of your teeth

11. Hell is other people.

12. God helps those who help themselves.

13. The blind leading the blind

14. A cat that catches mice does not meow.

15. Every dog will have his day.

16. Sour grapes

17. Seventh heaven

18. Put words in his mouth

19. To fall flat on your face

20. If you come to a fork in the road, take it.

THE ORIGINS OF THE SUNDAY SCHOOL

What comes to mind when you think of Sunday school? Flannelgraphs? Graham crackers that have outlived their "sell by this date" date by about two years? Twelve verses of "If You're Happy and You Know It" (is it possible not to know if you are happy?), complete with motions? Whatever your memory, it is probably a far cry from the actual origins of the Sunday school movement.

☛ THE BIRTH OF THE SUNDAY SCHOOL

The person generally acknowledged as the father of the Sunday school movement was an Anglican layman named Robert Raikes, born in Gloucester, England, in 1736. Raikes was a well-to-do publisher and the editor of the *Gloucester Journal.* Though wealthy, Raikes had a real soft spot for the down and out, and years before founding the Sunday school, he was a strong advocate for prison reform in an age when people could be locked away for life for failure to repay small debts.

England, at that time, had no public school system. Watching very young poor children head for low-paying factory jobs while their counterparts from wealthier families went to school, Raikes was moved to action. He was convinced that the only way out of the poverty cycle for these children was education, and Sunday was the only day many of these poor children were free from the factories. So Raikes set up Sunday schools, he found teachers, and the children were taught elementary reading, writing and math skills. In this early stage, the only text used was the Bible, because almost every household had one. Soon adults as well as children were attending these schools.

The movement grew rapidly in England, and by the middle of the nineteenth century, it is estimated that 75 percent of the children of this laboring class were attendees at Sunday schools. Not only did these classes provide a chance to obtain religious education and basic literary and mathematical skills, they also paved the way to social respectability by teaching etiquette and social skills. All of this was accomplished outside denominational structures, with almost all the leadership and teaching provided by laypeople.

SUNDAY SCHOOL GOES TO AMERICA

When the Sunday school movement headed across the Atlantic to America, the basic interest in literacy remained, but the American version was much more direct in its evangelistic efforts. Several small Sunday school associations had sprung up in the northeastern part of the United States in the early part of the nineteenth century, but the American Sunday School Union (ASSU), formed in 1824 in Philadelphia, soon became the major force for the movement in this country.

The ASSU quickly started publishing books—short, simple ones for early readers and longer ones for teens and adults—to be loaned to the Sunday schools for learners who could not afford their own. At its height in the middle of the nineteenth century, the ASSU had almost one thousand different titles in print. As in England, the schools educated both children and their parents, but they eventually moved toward a graded curriculum that took into account different age groups and skill levels.

ROBERT RAIKES, THE HORSE

As the country expanded westward, the Sunday schools were often the first establishments on the frontier, providing education before the public schools arrived. One major figure in the frontier establishment of Sunday schools was Stephen Paxson. Paxson had a severe stuttering problem and was crippled and had not been allowed into any school as a child. Undeterred, he taught himself to read, and then set out to spread both the gospel of Jesus and the gospel of literacy. Going from place to place on a horse he named "Robert Raikes" (in those days, you knew you had arrived if you had a horse named after you; things were less promising if you only had naming rights to the back quarter of the horse), he traveled 100,000 miles, planting Sunday schools wherever he went.

In about twenty-five years, records indicate, he organized over 1,300 such schools, with almost 100,000 people enrolled (or about one person per mile traveled).

While some denominations formed their own Sunday school unions, the ASSU remained by far the largest such group. It was quite notable in its nondenominational character, with all publications requiring approval of a board that consisted of at least one member from Baptist, Methodist, Congregational, Episcopal, Presbyterian, Lutheran and Reformed Dutch denominations (with no more than three members from any of these groups allowed). Over the years, the ASSU Board included several very prominent Americans, including George Washington's nephew, Bushrod Washington, who took over residence at Mount Vernon when his uncle died, and Francis Scott Key, who wrote the lyrics for "The Star-Spangled Banner."

The original structure and shape of the Sunday school movement began to change rapidly toward the end of the nineteenth century for a number of reasons—the widespread proliferation of public education and parochial schools as the frontiers were pushed back, the devastating effects of the Civil War, and denominational bickering. Nevertheless, the present-day United States was shaped in large part by the educational emphasis and the evangelistic efforts of the early Sunday school movement.

DID YOU KNOW?

Out of Africa

Tertullian, Cyril of Alexandria, Augustine, Athanasius and Cyprian are all important Christian theologians who lived prior to A.D. 500. In addition, they were all from the continent of Africa.

THEY'VE GOT YOU COVERED

In the Roman Catholic tradition, the saints intercede with God on behalf of various locales, occupations or conditions. With almost five thousand saints, virtually any situation one can conceive of is covered, especially since saints have patronage over several areas.

Some tasks of the patron saints are familiar to many, such as St. Christopher, protector of drivers and travelers, or St. Jude Thaddeus, patron of lost causes (including the Chicago Cubs). Other areas of patronage, however, are more unique and less well known. St. Julian the Hospitaller, for example, is the patron saint of carnival and circus workers (including jugglers). If carnival work seems a remnant of the past, the fact that St. Isidore of Seville is the patron saint of computer users and the Internet provides confidence that everything is up to date in Vatican City.

Just as every occupation seems saintly blessed, it is also difficult to conceive of a condition for which one cannot receive intercession. St. Fiacre is the patron saint of hemorrhoids and venereal disease, St. Vitus, a favorite among college students, is patron saint against oversleeping, and St. Drogo is the patron of unattractive people. St. Bibiana intercedes for those suffering from hangovers and insanity and is also the patron saint for the city of Los Angeles, a connection that seems to be more than simple coincidence.

While this is only a brief sampling, the range here should assure you that regardless of what you are facing in life, the saints have you covered.

PULLING OUT ALL THE STOPS

When people think about church music, many associate it closely with the venerable pipe organ. In the past, and still commonly today, you just didn't build a large church without one. However, the pipe organ already had a history that stretched back over a thousand years before they started showing up in churches. Here's some of the story about the evolution of the pipe organ, with a few quirky facts thrown in.

ORGAN ORIGINS

Ctesibius of Alexandria, who lived somewhere around the middle of the third century B.C., is generally credited with the invention of the pipe organ. These early models were originally called a hydraulis because water pressure (hydraulics, get it?) was used to create a steady source of air pressure. The sound of this organ, then as now, was generated by the air passing through the pipes. These early organs had only one sound per note and were played by levers rather than keys on a manual.

The hydraulis became an instant hit with the Greeks and, later, the Romans. The emperor Nero is reported to have been a hydraulis player, and it was more likely he played this instrument than a fiddle while Rome burned. Because of the volume that it could produce, it became a popular musical accompaniment for large-scale events such as the circuses and games of the Roman era. However, as the Roman Empire came apart at the seams, the pipe organ disappeared for about three centuries in the Western world. It was reintroduced to the West when Emperor Constantius shipped one to Pepin the Short (yep, that's a real person), King of the Franks, in the eighth century.

The first reference to a pipe organ in a church only appears around the year 900, but once they got in, the popularity of the instrument in churches grew steadily. There were a few bumps along the way, however. When the Puritans took control of England during the seventeenth century, they had a very dim view of organs in churches, and destroyed many of the church organs in that country.

One of the bigger competitors to the church pipe organ emerged in the 1930s with the invention of the Hammond electronic organ. Because it was cheaper and took up far less space than a pipe organ, the Hammond organ made a serious dent in the pipe organ business. The pipe organ builders did get a minor victory in 1938, however, when the courts ordered the Hammond Company to stop advertising that its electronic organ was the sonic equal to pipe organs.

☞ EVOLUTION TOWARD THE MODERN PIPE ORGAN

As people tinkered with the organ, they began to improve on the original design. In the second century, bellows began to replace hydraulic pressure as the air source for organs. Keys replaced levers to activate notes, and over time the range of pitches increased to a standard keyboard of sixty-one notes (a piano has eighty-eight) and thirty-two pedals. It also became popular to combine several different pipes with one note, which added color and depth to the sound produced. Nevertheless, each note could produce only one kind of sound until the invention of the stop in the late fifteenth century, which allowed the organist to shut off the air to a complete set of pipes (or rank). The use of stops greatly enhanced both the range of volume and sounds available from a single instrument. This explains the origin of the phrase "pulling out all the stops," where the organist opens everything up and shakes the stained glass. About the same time stops were invented, pedalboards were added to organs so the subwoofer on your stereo gets a bit more exercise.

THINKING BIG

The which-is-the-biggest question always generates arguments, and the issue of which pipe organ is the largest is no exception. The *Guinness Book of World Records* identifies the organ in the Atlantic City Convention Center as the world's biggest. It also gets credit as the loudest musical instrument in existence, which can be helpful information in case you need to drown out some bagpipe "music." The main console for this organ has seven manuals (or keyboards) and is surrounded by enough knobs, couplers and pedals to make an experienced 747 pilot curl up into a fetal position.

If that's too overwhelming, this organ has a "portable" console with a mere five manuals. Unfortunately the smaller console is disconnected and on display elsewhere in the building, which is probably not the reason they made it portable. *Guinness* lists the number of pipes in this organ at 33,114 (455 ranks), although some claim that this number is about a thousand too high. When you have this many pipes (the smallest is only a quarter-inch long), it's a bit tricky to get an accurate count. NASCAR fans will be impressed by the fact that the blowers that power this baby weigh in at just under one thousand horsepower.

Alas, this massive organ is in a rather sad state of repair and "only" about 140 of the ranks are operational. Thus, many count the Wanamaker Organ of Philadelphia as the world's biggest. This pipe organ is located, of all places, in the middle of the Lord & Taylor department store. Definitely a new twist on department store "Muzak."™

The Wanamaker was built in 1904 for the St. Louis World's Fair and required thirteen freight cars to ship it to its current home in Philly. The original organ had "only" about ten thousand pipes and was deemed underpowered for the space. This deficiency was taken care of by adding another eighteen thousand pipes. Even if the Wanamaker Organ isn't the biggest, it has something the Atlantic City organ doesn't: its own gift shop.

The world's largest church organ is also a matter of controversy. Most put the pipe organ of First Congregational Church in Los Angeles, which has over twenty thousand individual pipes, at the top of the list. The Cadet Chapel at West Point comes equipped with an organ of about the same size. However, some argue that you only have a real church if the building has been duly consecrated by a bishop in apostolic succession. With this definition, the biggest church organ is in St. Stephen's Cathedral in Passau, Germany. The all-glass Crystal Cathedral (Robert Schuller's church) also has a whopper (sixth on the all-time list), but no official word on whether it has enough oomph to shatter the windows. In the specialty organ category, St. Joseph Church in the Philippines claims the title of "largest bamboo organ." This instrument is two centuries old and has 174 bamboo pipes and 22 stops.

A REALLY BIG LITTLE NATION

What sovereign nation has a land mass of less than 0.2 square miles (just over one hundred acres) and a population of under one thousand? The vast majority of the residents own absolutely nothing, but the assets of this country make it by far the world's wealthiest nation per capita. Even with this great wealth, the nation produces no goods and has no exports. Most of its income is derived from donations, supplemented by museum admission fees, sales of souvenirs to tourists, and stamp and coin sales. It also has probably the most highly educated citizens of any nation in the world.

This state has a military force of about a hundred soldiers, all mercenaries. What this army lacks in size and weaponry (standard issue weapons are a large sword and a halberd, a ten-foot-long pole with an ax blade and spear point at the top) it makes up for in style, sporting snazzy bright orange, yellow, red and blue uniforms and metal helmets with red plumes. Crammed into this micronation, a visitor will find seven radio stations, one TV station and a newspaper that publishes in several languages. It has its own international country code for telephone calls (39), Internet suffix, formal diplomatic relations with virtually every nation on earth, and permanent observer status at the UN.

Got it figured out yet? Just a couple more hints. The head of this nation has been appointed for life and is an individual whose name is immediately identifiable almost everywhere in the world. The country is the only one in the world whose population is 100 percent Christian. The nation: Vatican City, or, more precisely, the Holy See.

While most people are very aware of Vatican City's existence as an enclave surrounded by the city of Rome, many do not realize that it is a separate, sovereign nation. The Holy See's current borders came into existence in 1929. Throughout the nineteenth century, the Papal States in Italy were absorbed by the Kingdom of Italy, culminating in the seizure of Rome, which had been under the church's political control, in 1870. After six decades of dispute about the ownership of Rome, Italy (then ruled by Mussolini) and the Holy See signed three treaties in 1929 that, among other things, designated Vatican City as an independent state.

Contained within the Holy See is St. Peter's Square and St. Peter's Basilica, undoubtedly the most famous church in the world; the Vatican Museums, which contain some of the most priceless art and artifacts in the world; the Vatican Library; the well-known Sistine Chapel; apartments housing the pope and other church officials; and a barracks for the military force, the Swiss Guard.

The official language of the Holy See is Latin, although much of the business of the country is carried on in Italian. German is used by the Swiss Guard. Only about a thousand people hold Vatican citizenship, almost all of them clergy. No one is a citizen of the Holy See by birth (for what should be obvious reasons) and all residents hold dual citizenships, including the current head of the state, Pope Benedict XVI, who has both German and Vatican citizenships. (However, the pope also accepted citizenship and a passport from the city of Bethlehem in June 2005, becoming its first citizen after it was declared an open city.)

With a country occupied almost exclusively by clergy, one might expect the crime rate to be pretty low. However, given the constant flood of tourists, Vatican City's crime rate is almost off the charts when calculated on a per citizen basis. Pickpockets and purse snatchers are the main culprits.

Though tiny in size and population, The Holy See administers and directs the spiritual affairs for one billion Roman Catholics worldwide, one-sixth of the planet's population and about half the world's Christians.

OH, SUSANNA

When you think about it, history leaves us with information about very few of the people who have ever populated this planet. The vast majority of people are completely forgotten a few years after their death. (How's that for an upbeat way to start things?) However, among all these forgotten lives, there are incredible stories of strength, faith and the amazing ability to overcome odds. Who knows how many of these inspiring biographies have been lost through the years? Every now and then, though, we hear about someone who lived in the background but indirectly did something that changed the world in a profound way. This is exactly what happened with a woman named Susanna.

If you consider the factors that give a person the chance to be noticed in life, Susanna did not have a promising beginning. When you are the youngest of twenty-five children, as was Susanna, it is easy to get lost in the shuffle. At age nineteen, she married an Anglican pastor and they were chronically poor for their entire life. Her husband, Samuel, worked hard at being a good minister, but his harsh personality led to frequent clashes with his parishioners as well as tensions with Susanna, who also had strong opinions about things.

In fact, the two were separated for a year when they had a deep political disagreement. Susanna refused to say "Amen" to Samuel's prayer for King William, a monarch she considered to be illegitimately seated on England's throne. When she would not back down, Samuel took an opportunity to serve in London. As if the separation itself were not enough, Susanna was left to care for their eight children by herself.

Reconciliation finally came a year later through two different factors. First, King William died and Queen Anne, a monarch acceptable to both Samuel and Susanna, ascended to the throne. Second, Samuel and Susanna's house burned down. Samuel returned home, and the next year another child was born, followed by yet another, bringing the total to ten. And this just counts those who lived past infancy. In all, Susanna bore somewhere between seventeen and nineteen children in nineteen years.

Susanna took her motherly duties seriously. She taught each child to read at the age of five and kept a close eye on their education. Susanna kept an even closer eye on their spiritual instruction. She would rise before anyone in the house, spend an hour in Scripture and devotional reading herself, then begin lessons for the children with the singing of hymns. In addition, Susanna set aside an hour every week for each child and used this time to encourage them in their faith.

One event that helps complete our portrait of Susanna's spirit occurred when Samuel had to travel to London for an extended period. Susanna, during this time, would gather her family and read sermons and devotional works in an evening worship. Soon others joined—a lot of others. These evening meetings grew to two hundred attendees, and the parsonage overflowed. The curate left in charge during Samuel's absence became jealous because these informal assemblies drew more than his Sunday morning services. He wrote to Samuel complaining that such meetings constituted illegal religious meetings (and he may well have been correct about this).

Samuel wrote to Susanna suggesting that the meetings be ended. She refused because she could see no wrong in services that increased the religious devotion of those who attended. Again the curate complained to Samuel, and again he tried to put a stop to things. Susanna finally wrote, "If after all this you think fit to dissolve this assembly, do not tell me you *desire* me to do it, for that will not satisfy my conscience: but send your *positive command* in such full and express terms as may absolve me from all guilt and punishment for neglecting this opportunity for doing good when you and I shall appear before the great and awful tribunal of our Lord Jesus Christ." Well, if you put it like that. By the way, the meetings continued until Samuel returned from London.

Seven years after the fire that demolished the rectory, Samuel and Susanna once again watched their house burn. This time, however, their five-year-old son, the son born after their reconciliation, was trapped in the burning house. The flames were so intense that no one was able to enter the house to rescue him. Just before the roof collapsed, the young boy appeared in a window and was pulled to safety. After this event, Susanna was sure that God had a special task in mind for the young boy, whose escape was so narrow that he would later refer to himself as "a brand plucked from the burning."

Susanna's intuition proved to be true. This young boy, John Wesley, would later spark a revolution that would make a profound and long-lasting spiritual impact across the world.

"KUM BA YAH"

Almost no one over the age of thirty escaped a camp without singing "Kum Ba Yah." If they didn't get you at church camp, they nailed you at Scout camp with it.

☞ "KUM BA YAH" MEETS CHURCH CAMP

How the song made its journey from Negro Spiritual to omnipres-ent camp song is something of a mystery, but combine a melody with hook, a minimal requirement of four easy guitar chords and the potential for endless variations on the verses, and you have the stuff of which camp-song legends are created. In fact, the connec-tion between "Kum Ba Yah" and camp is so strong that there is even a Camp Kum Ba Yah in Virginia.

The phrase *kum ba yah* means "Come by here." Some have identified the language of these words as Gullah, a combination of African dialects and English used in the coastal areas of Georgia and South Carolina in the eighteenth and nineteenth centuries.

As if anyone needs to be reminded, the basic song is

Kum ba yah, My Lord. Kum ba yah.
Kum ba yah, My Lord. Kum ba yah.
Kum ba yah, My Lord. Kum ba yah.
O Lord, Kum ba yah.

Once you get past the initial verse, all bets are off, since the tune allows for an infinite number of permutations, but the most common church-camp variations are

Someone's crying, Lord. Kum ba yah.
Someone's singing, Lord. Kum ba yah.
Someone's praying, Lord. Kum ba yah.

☞ "KUM BA YAH" MEETS SCOUT CAMP

If your background is in Scouting, however, a more familiar form
may be the Scout Law version in which the attributes included in
the Scout Law are wedged into the song, as in

A scout is trustworthy, Lord. Kum ba yah.
A scout is loyal, Lord. Kum ba yah.
A scout is helpful, Lord. Kum ba yah.

. . . and so on until you get through all the ideal characteristics
of your local Scout.

☞ "KUM BA YAH" MEETS POLITICAL CORRECTNESS

For those who never want to hear the song again, our current cli-
mate of political correctness may offer relief. At a Florida Boys &
Girls Club day camp, eight-year-old Samantha Schultz was not allowed to sing "Kum Ba Yah" for the rest of the campers because it
contained the highly offensive word *Lord*. As Randy Bouck, the director, put it, "We just can't allow any religious songs. You have to
check your religion at the door."

If you are one of the lucky few who could read this section without getting the melody of "Kum Ba Yah" lodged in your head for
the rest of the day, I have only this to say . . . "It's a Small World
After All."

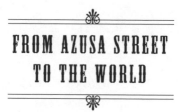

FROM AZUSA STREET TO THE WORLD

By almost any measure, it would be hard to dispute the claim that the most significant development in the Christian world during the twentieth century was the birth and amazing growth of the Pentecostal/charismatic movement. From humble and unremarkable beginnings at a small Bible school in Topeka, Kansas, this movement has exploded into a worldwide phenomenon whose adherents now number in the neighborhood of 500,000,000 people.

A NEW TAKE ON HOLY SPIRIT BAPTISM

The theological groundwork for Pentecostalism had been prepared by late-nineteenth-century holiness groups, which taught the idea of a "second blessing" in the Christian life, often connecting this with the "baptism of the Holy Spirit." However, at this time, the second blessing/baptism in the Holy Spirit concept was linked with spiritual holiness or perfection, not speaking in tongues.

In 1900, Charles Fox Parham, a former Methodist pastor, started The College at Bethel, a Bible school in Topeka, Kansas. In the closing days of that year, the students had been studying the New Testament idea of Holy Spirit baptism, and on New Year's Day, 1901, Agnes Ozmen, one of the school's students, spoke in tongues. Two days later, twelve other students also reported the same experience. Parham saw this as a sign that the new century would be the time of worldwide evangelism, and set off on an extensive tour of revival meetings throughout the midwestern states to spread the message.

🐦 PENTECOST COMES TO L.A.

In 1903, Parham was again teaching in a small Bible school, this time in Houston, Texas. A young man who heard his views about the baptism of the Holy Spirit, William Seymour, was convinced by Parham's ideas. A few weeks later, Seymour moved to Los Angeles where he had been recommended to a small Holiness church. His first sermon on Acts 2:4 ("All of them were filled with the Holy Spirit and began to speak in other languages, as the Spirit gave them ability") struck a resonant chord with the congregation, but not the pastor, who banned Seymour from the church.

Without a church to pastor, Seymour stayed with some members of the congregation and began to hold Bible studies at their home on Bonnie Brae Street. In the next few days, several participants received the gift of tongues. Word spread, and the group grew out of the house and onto the porch. When the porch collapsed because of the number of people, they rented a former AME Church, which, for the past several years had fallen into disrepair and was being used as a livery and storage building. The address of this wood-frame structure was to become the most famous in Pentecostal history: 312 Azusa Street. Boards were set atop old nail kegs in place of pews, and the services began.

🐦 "WEIRD BABEL OF TONGUES"

News of an amazing revival reached the media, and on the morning of April 18, 1906 (the same morning the massive earthquake hit San Francisco), the headlines of the *Los Angeles Daily News* read "WEIRD BABEL OF TONGUES, New Sect of Fanatics is Breaking Loose, Wild Scene Last Night on Azusa Street, Gurgle of Wordless Talk by a Sister." For the next three years, the revival continued at Azusa Street. Every day of the week, three services, and often more, were conducted. They started in the morning and often went deep into the night.

People came from all over the world to see what was happening at Azusa Street, and the movement spread rapidly. Seymour began to publish a newsletter, *The Apostolic Faith,* which he distributed for free. At its height, it had fifty thousand subscribers. The Pentecostal message spread rapidly, both in the United States and overseas.

☞ A FORGOTTEN ASPECT OF AZUSA STREET

While the account of Pentecostal beginnings at Azusa Street is an important one, there is a story within the story that is also very significant, but not heard as often. When Seymour heard the teachings of Parham back in 1903, he listened from the hallway. You see, Seymour was African American, and was not allowed to sit in the classroom because of his race.

From the beginning of the movement in Los Angeles, race was not allowed to be a barrier. Blacks and whites met together in the house meetings on Bonnie Brae Street. Photos of the meetings at the Azusa Street Mission give a vision of something extremely rare today, but unheard of in the highly segregated society of the early twentieth century. All worshiped together—whites, blacks, Asians, Hispanics. The staff of the ministry was similarly integrated. A witness of the revivals, Frank Bartleman, wrote, "At Azusa Street, the color line was washed away in the Blood." What is more, the leaders were steered by the belief that if the Holy Spirit does not discriminate when it falls on believers, then neither should they. Thus, women were given full ministry roles in the Azusa Street revival.

By many estimates, 25 percent of the world's Christians today can be identified as Pentecostal or charismatic, and their numbers are growing faster than any segment of the Christian world today. If you go to the site of the Azusa Street meeting house today in downtown Los Angeles, the livery is long gone. All you will find are two modest plaques, one describing what occurred at the site and another honoring the work of Seymour, small indicators that the San Francisco earthquake was not California's only seismic event on April 18, 1906.

THE HOLY LAND EXPERIENCE

Had it up to your ears with Mickey and his high-priced Disney pals? Got a severe case of "been there, done that" with the Universal Studios theme park? Move over Epcot, the Holy Land Experience theme park is in town—Orlando, that is. Now you don't have to fly halfway around the world to experience the Holy Land. The Holy Land Experience is right here in the good old U.S.A.

☛ THE HOLY LAND COMES TO AMERICA

For seventeen dollars, or twelve dollars for those who have not reached bar mitzvah age (that's twelve years old, for you Gentiles out there), you can gain admission to what the owners call a "living museum" that re-creates such biblical structures as the Temple of the Great King and caves that are replicas of the Qumran caverns where the Dead Sea Scrolls were found. The six-story Temple of the Great King is actually a theater, where visitors can view a twenty-five-minute whirlwind trip through the Bible with a film titled *The Seed of Promise.*

While strolling through the fifteen-acre park, you can take in a passion play at the Calvary Garden Tomb or do a bit of window shopping at The Old Scroll Shop or Methuselah's Mosaics. Along the way, you are likely to be greeted with an enthusiastic "Shalom" by "cast members" dressed as shepherds, Jewish priests or Roman centurions (it's a bit spooky to hear a centurion say "Shalom"). Some of the cast members will pause to tell Bible stories connected with particular points in the park. (No mention whether the story of Jesus overturning the money-changers' tables is recounted inside the temple.)

Since its opening in February 2001, the Holy Land Experience has made a significant addition to the park. An 18,000-square-foot museum, called The Scriptorium, has been opened. Modeled on a fourth-century Byzantine architectural style, The Scriptorium contains what is one of the best privately owned collections of ancient Near Eastern artifacts in the world. Cuneiform tablets, papyrus scrolls, ancient manuscripts and other artifacts are displayed with information about the settings in which they originated.

If you work up an appetite on your Holy Land trek, you can stop by the Oasis Palms Café and pick up a Goliath Burger for $5.95 or a Bedouin Beef Wrap for just a buck more (perhaps Manna-coti could be added to the menu at a later date?), then wash it all down with a Thirsty-Camel Cooler for $2.50. Not too bad as theme-park meal prices go. However, you may find it a bit difficult to stay in the spirit of things since you can see an outside-the-park 7-Eleven sign from the Oasis Palms, especially when you start thinking about two corn dogs for a dollar and a Super Big Gulp® for half what you shelled out for the Thirsty-Camel Cooler. If it seems a bit of a step down to be experiencing the Holy Land in Florida, it might cheer you up to know that most of the products sold in the park's Jerusalem Street Market are imported from Israel.

☞ PROTESTING THE HOLY LAND

As you might guess, a religious theme park cannot open without controversy. The executive director of the Holy Land Experience is Marv Rosenthal. Rosenthal was born a Jew but is now a Baptist minister who heads an organization called Zion's Hope. The fact that Zion's Hope is a group that seeks to bring the gospel to Jews caught the attention of Irv Rubin, head of the Jewish Defense League. He accused the group of "soul-stealing," and promised a massive protest on opening day. The "massive protest," in the end, consisted of Rubin and a friend holding up a protest banner. Nevertheless, the whole event was deemed worthy of coverage by CNN, the *New York Times* and even the BBC (being the international affair that it was). The media coverage did wonders for opening day at the park, which had to turn away twice as many cars as its lot would hold.

While things got off to a good start for the Holy Land Experience, all did not turn out well for Rubin, our intrepid protester. He was arrested ten months later for plotting to bomb a mosque and the office of an Arab American congressman. A year later, he attempted suicide by slashing his throat with a razor, and fell over a railing to a concrete floor twenty feet below. He was declared brain-dead and died a week later.

In any case, if the turmoil in the Middle East makes you a bit reluctant to head for Israel, the Holy Land Experience offers a taste of Jerusalem, circa A.D. 66, with the world's largest indoor model of the city. Then, wrap up your big day with a milk-and-honey ice cream cone as you head back to the parking lot.

FISH OUT OF WATER

No doubt you have witnessed the "great bumper sticker fish debate" as you cruise the streets and freeways. On one car, you see a fish symbol. On the next, an evolved two-legged fish (heading the opposite direction) with "Darwin" written across the body is seen. Then, as the profound conclusion to the debate, you get the big "Truth" fish swallowing the "Darwin" fish.

A good percentage of people are aware that the fish symbol has been used by Christians to identify themselves to the world, but it is less commonly known how this symbol came about. The origin of this association probably goes back to the second century A.D., when Greek (the language of the New Testament) was still a language that almost everyone understood, even if it was not their mother tongue. The letters often seen inside the fish symbol today—iota, chi, theta, upsilon and sigma—spell out the Greek word for "fish" *(ichthys)*. This combination of letters forms an acrostic for *Iesous Christos Theou Hyios Soter,* or in English translation, "Jesus Christ, God's Son, Savior."

There are several possibilities for explaining how this symbol became so prominent at an early stage of the church's existence. Some of Jesus' disciples were fishermen, and Jesus, in calling them to follow him, invited them to be "fishers of men" (Matthew 4:19). Several of Jesus' miracles involved fish, such as the multiplication of the loaves and fishes (Matthew 14:15-21) or the great haul of fish (Luke 5:3-11). Also, part of Jesus' meal with his disciples following his resurrection consisted of fish (John 21:9-14).

Fish symbols are found in the catacombs (burial caves) of Rome in the early part of the second century A.D., and these may well mark the graves of Christians. The first written reference to the symbol comes about A.D. 150 from Clement of Alexandria, who recommends that Christians using signets to seal business documents have doves or fish engraved upon them. He does not explain why they should use the fish symbol, which probably indicates that the fish was already recognized as a common Christian emblem by that time. Around 200, Tertullian uses the symbolism of the fish to speak of the importance of baptism when he says, "But we, being little fishes, as Jesus Christ is our great Fish, begin our life in the water, and only while we abide in the water are we safe and sound" *(On Baptism)*.

Some have argued that the fish symbol was used in the early days of the church's life when persecution of Christians was common. An old story says that a Christian, upon meeting a person whose religious allegiance was unknown, would draw an arc on the ground with their foot or walking stick. If the unknown person would then draw the opposing arc, completing the picture of the fish, both would know it was safe to speak to each other of their faith without fear of persecution.

Whether the story of the fish as a secret symbol is anything but a fish tale is difficult to determine. In any case, if you check out the phone directories and bumpers today, it is clear that the fish remains a common way for Christians to make themselves known to others. In fact, there is even a Christian radio station that identifies itself as "The Fish," which obviously would not be a very positive association without insider knowledge of the symbolism.

GREAT OPENING LINES

Your Bible includes a number of elements that the earliest readers of Scripture would not have found in theirs. For example, as previously mentioned, they had no chapter or verse designations to help them locate a specific passage. In addition, the original biblical manuscripts did not have titles for specific books. So how did they know what they were reading? Early readers of the Hebrew Bible would identify books by the first word, so when they unrolled the scroll containing the book we now call Genesis, the first word they would see was *bereshith*, a Hebrew term usually translated in English as "In the beginning." Thus, they referred to the book simply as *Bereshith*.

I'm going to make things a bit easier for you. You will get not just the first word, but the entire opening verse (in some cases, I have used verse two, since the first verse often includes the name of the book, which takes the sport out of it). Your job is to match this opening verse with the book of the Bible it comes from. Some will be familiar, but others are more challenging. It's even in English (the NRSV, to be exact).

1.___ "This happened in the days of   a. Hebrews
       Ahasuerus, the same Ahasuerus who
       ruled over one hundred and twenty-
       seven provinces from India to
       Ethiopia."

2.___ "In the days when the judges ruled,   b. Song of Solomon
there was a famine in the land, and a
certain man of Bethlehem in Judah
went to live in the country of Moab,
he and his wife and two sons."

3.___ "Long ago God spoke to our ances-   c. Ruth
tors in many and various ways by the
prophets."

4.___ "In the beginning when God created   d. Psalms
the heavens and the earth."

5.___ "I will utterly sweep away everything   e. 1 Chronicles
from the face of the earth, says the
LORD" (verse 2).

6.___ "In the beginning was the Word, and   f. Gospel of John
the Word was with God, and the
Word was God."

7.___ "Adam, Seth, Enosh" (That really is   g. Esther
the entire first verse. Not enough?
Here's the complete second verse to
help you out: "Kenan, Mahalalel,
Jared").

8.___ "The elder to the elect lady and her   h. Acts of the
children, whom I love in the truth,   Apostles
and not only I but also all who know
the truth."

9.___ "Let him kiss me with the kisses of his   i. 2 John
mouth! For your love is better than
wine" (verse 2, technically).

10.___ "In the thirtieth year, in the fourth   j. Ezekiel
        month, on the fifth day of the month,
        as I was among the exiles by the
        river Chebar, the heavens were
        opened, and I saw visions of God."

11.___ "Happy are those who do not follow   k. Genesis
        the advice of the wicked, or take the
        path that sinners tread, or sit in the
        seat of scoffers."

12.___ "In the first book, Theophilus, I   l. Zephaniah
        wrote about all that Jesus did and
        taught from the beginning."

BONUS QUESTION:

You may have noticed that none of the epistles of Paul are listed above. That is because each of the letters attributed to him begin with the same word—*Paul*—which takes a bit of the challenge out of things. Since Martin Luther would be very disappointed if we left Paul out completely, the bonus question is, Which of Paul's letters begins with the following opening verse?

"Paul an apostle—sent neither by human commission nor from human authorities, but through Jesus Christ and God the Father, who raised him from the dead—"

See page 162 for answers.

EXECUTION BY BAPTISM

It took Protestantism just slightly more than five years to achieve a dubious benchmark: the first martyrdom of a Protestant at the hands of other Protestants.

The reform efforts of Ulrich Zwingli in Zurich had won over an energetic and bright follower named Felix Manz. Over time, however, Manz became convinced that Zwingli's reforms stopped short of what Scripture required. In particular, he believed that the concept of salvation by faith was inconsistent with the practice of infant baptism, and entered into debate over this issue with Zwingli before the Zurich council.

The council sided with Zwingli on the baptism issue, but Manz was not deterred. His preaching drew thousands to his position and also led to his arrest on a number of occasions. In 1525 a decisive step was taken when one of Manz's associates, Conrad Grebel, rebaptized a former Catholic priest, who immediately rebaptized several others. This practice earned the group the label of "Anabaptists" (*ana* = "again"). It also led the Zurich council to make these adult baptisms punishable by death.

Manz, not quite thirty years old yet, was arrested for participating in rebaptisms and sentenced to death in a manner designed to fit the crime. On January 7, 1527, Manz's hands were bound and pulled behind his knees. He was taken to the middle of the Limmat River by boat and thrown in the water—to drown.

Over the next several years, many of Manz's fellow Anabaptists were executed in a similar manner by both Protestants and Catholics.

MICHELANGELO AND THE SISTINE CHAPEL

One of the favorite destinations for lovers of Christian art is the Sistine Chapel. The chapel itself was built to mirror the dimensions given for the Old Testament temple, about 131 feet by 43 feet, and was completed in 1483. Here the art does not just hang on the walls. The walls (and the ceiling) of the Sistine Chapel *are* art.

The Sistine Chapel's walls are covered with paintings by a veritable who's who of Renaissance artists, but the two most famous works—the chapel ceiling and the *Last Judgment*—are the creations of Michelangelo (in his pre-Teenage Mutant Ninja Turtle days). The choice of Michelangelo for this work was rather improbable. He had done almost no painting prior to his commission to do the ceiling, and he really did not like painting. He saw himself as a sculptor instead. However, popes can be rather persuasive, and Pope Julius II finally prevailed on Michelangelo to take the job of repainting the Sistine Chapel's ceiling (originally it had been painted with stars against the background of a blue sky).

THE CHAPEL CEILING

Painting ceilings is never easy work, and this particular job had several daunting challenges. First, it was over sixty feet high. Michelangelo nixed an original idea to suspend scaffolding from the ceiling since that would involve making holes in the ceiling it-self, which would remain when his work was complete. He de-signed scaffolding that could be attached to the walls, and arched it in the middle to match the curve of the ceiling.

Even with the scaffolding in place, he still had the uncomfortable task of painting above his head. He did not, as Charlton Heston portrayed it in *The Agony and the Ecstasy*, paint while lying on his back, however. Another big problem was that the early type of plaster used on the ceil-ing got moldy, so his assistant came up with a new plaster formula and redid the entire ceil-ing with a recipe that is still in use.

The original plan for the ceiling of the Sis-tine Chapel was a painting of the twelve apos-tles. When Michelangelo was done, how-ever, there were more than three hundred figures and the central panels consisted of nine Old Testament scenes that take us from the creation of Adam to an intoxicated post-flood Moses. The entire area measures almost five thousand square feet, and Michelangelo himself did almost all the painting, although apprentices did some of the background painting and a few minor figures. He also had a number of assistants who pre-pared and transported the materials to him. Work on the ceiling went on for more than four years, and was completed in 1512.

☛ THE *LAST JUDGMENT* AND THE JUDGMENT UPON THE *LAST JUDGMENT*

A couple of decades later, Michelangelo was called to Rome again by Pope Paul III, who commissioned him to complete a massive fresco on the entire wall behind the altar of the Sistine Chapel. This was originally supposed to be a picture of the resurrection of

Jesus, but the final product turned out to be the final judgment, with the blessed rising to meet Jesus on the right side and the condemned heading the other direction on the left. This mural took almost seven years to complete, but it generated considerable controversy before it was ever finished. The problem was that many of the figures were done as nudes. In response to complaints, Michelangelo replied that bodies do not take their clothes with them to heaven.

One who was less than impressed with the *Last Judgment* was Biagio da Cesena, the pope's master of ceremonies, who contended that the fresco full of exposed genitalia was more fitting for a bathhouse than the pope's chapel. It's never a good idea to irritate an artist, and Michelangelo got his revenge by painting Cesena's face on the figure of Minos, the god of the underworld. One legend has it that when Cesena complained about his unflattering inclusion in the fresco, the pope said he had no jurisdiction over hell. So Cesena's likeness remains to this day.

Things did not end there. When Michelangelo died (fourteen years after the *Last Judgment* was completed), the decision was made to hire a painter to cover up all the exposed naughty parts. The artist chosen for this task was Daniele da Volterra, who painted *braghe* (Italian skivvies) on several of the most prominent nude figures. This is often referred to as the "Fig-Leaf Campaign."

In 1980 a fourteen-year restoration process began on the Sistine Chapel to brighten up the paintings that had been dulled by age and candle smoke. One of the questions was whether the *braghe* painted by Volterra should be removed. The final compromise was that many of the "draperies" that had been added to other figures in subsequent centuries would be removed, but those provided by Volterra would stay. If you are distressed by this violation of artistic freedom, an uncensored copy of the *Last Judgment* can be seen at the Capodimonte Museum in Naples.

MORE THAN JUST BELL-RINGERS

What comes to mind when you think about the Salvation Army? Soup kitchens, the Salvation Army Band (with a very complete tambourine section), used clothing pickups and, of course, the shiny red Christmas donation kettles with the omnipresent bell-ringers around the holiday season. A lot of people, however, don't realize that the Salvation Army is also a vibrant Christian denominational group (what part of "salvation" don't you understand?), although it has a rather different structure than many such organizations.

☛ WILLIAM, CATHERINE AND A NEW ARMY

It all started in England with William and Catherine Booth. At thirteen, William worked as an apprentice to a pawnbroker to support his mother and siblings. This experience made him sensitive to the pitiful plight of the impoverished. After his apprenticeship, he became a traveling Methodist minister. He met Catherine Mumford while preaching at her church, and they were eventually married.

From the beginning, Catherine was an integral part of his ministry. In fact, while she was rather shy and never felt completely comfortable speaking in public, she became a powerful preacher in her own right and was convinced that women should have equal opportunities in ministry. Thus, from the beginning, all ranks within the Salvation Army structure have been open to women, and two women have held the rank of General, commanding the worldwide organization.

In 1865, while preaching in London's deeply impoverished East End, the Booths knew that they had found their calling. They began "The Christian Mission" to minister to the destitute people. The early years were very difficult. Meetings were frequently interrupted by hecklers, and stones and fireworks were often thrown at Booth while he preached.

In 1878, The Christian Mission changed its name to the Salvation Army, and the image of a Christian army mobilized against sin proved to be very powerful. The work of the Salvation Army spread rapidly, and by the time William Booth died, it was active in over fifty countries. Today the Salvation Army is at work in over one hundred different countries with about seventeen thousand active full-time ministers (called "officers") engaged in Christian service and over a million adult members (called "senior soldiers") in the denomination.

The Booths never intended for the Salvation Army to become a separate church. However, when people were converted, these new Christians would be shunned by established churches because they almost all came from the dregs of society. Understanding that the new converts required a lot of nurture, Salvation Army churches, called corps, began to spring up everywhere they had evangelistic missions. These converts from the poorest urban centers were so effectively groomed in the faith that they comprised the vast majority of the Salvation Army Officers for many decades.

☞ THE ARMY ATTACKED, AND THE ARMY'S COUNTERATTACK

Because of their commitment to make the gospel heard wherever conditions were the most dire, early Salvationists would frequently hold evangelistic services in the streets. These were often rowdy affairs. Verbal abuse was heaped on them, and they were pelted with garbage, eggs and rocks by those who were annoyed by their calls to repentance. At times, they were met by violent mobs armed with clubs and knives, often organized by pub owners unhappy that some of their best customers had become Christians and dried out. Several Salvationists were killed by angry groups.

One novel approach to dealing with unruly crowds helps explain the origin of a distinctive tradition closely associated with this movement—the Salvation Army band. In 1878, Charles Fry, together with his three sons, put together a brass quartet that would drown out hecklers and draw attention to the street meetings. This was so effective that the use of bands became widespread. While the first groups played only arrangements of Christian music, soon they began to use secular tunes and put Christian lyrics with them. Today, music education is an important part of the Salvation Army's work, and almost every corps has a band and songster brigade (choir). At one time, the Salvation Army even had their own factory to manufacture band instruments, and they still hold the patent on the E-flat bass slide trombone, an instrument invented for their bands.

☞ THE SHINY RED CHRISTMAS KETTLE

While the Salvation Army had its roots in England, the Salvation Army Christmas kettle was born in America. In 1891 a Salvation Army captain, Joseph McFee, was looking for a way to provide meals for the homeless in San Francisco during the Christmas season. He remembered seeing a pot in Liverpool, England, called "Simpson's Pot," that passersby would toss loose change into. McFee put a pot at a ferry landing near Market Street, and the response was so phenomenal that by 1900 they were in use all over America. In fact, the Christmas kettle has gone international and is in use in several European countries, Chile and even Japan.

Each year, the Salvation Army provides aid to about five million Americans during the Thanksgiving and Christmas season. Almost half the money for this work comes from the coins and bills that find their way into the shiny red Christmas kettles whose locations are indicated by the sounds of the bell-ringers.

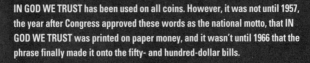

DID YOU KNOW?

"In God We Trust," Since 1957

The motto "IN GOD WE TRUST" did not appear on any U.S. money until 1864, when it was first inscribed on a two-cent piece. Since 1939, IN GOD WE TRUST has been used on all coins. However, it was not until 1957, the year after Congress approved these words as the national motto, that IN GOD WE TRUST was printed on paper money, and it wasn't until 1966 that the phrase finally made it onto the fifty- and hundred-dollar bills.

A CHURCH WITH NO NAME

What do you call a denomination that has no ordination, no sermons, no doctrinal statement, no paid staff, no printed materials at all except a hymnal, no buildings and no tax-exempt status? Actually, the people in this church would prefer that you not call it anything. That's what they do, or don't do. This denomination has no name. In fact, it thinks that naming a church is very unchurchlike. After all, they argue, the New Testament church didn't have a label, and it did pretty well for itself.

Just because you don't give your denominational group a name doesn't mean that others won't do it for you. As a result, outsiders have referred to this church by various labels, including Go Preachers, Workers, the No-Name Church or, most commonly, the Two-by-Twos (or 2x2). The latter comes from the group's practice of sending out members in pairs to evangelize.

The group started with the preaching of a Scottish lay evangelist, William Irvine. In 1901, Irvine started sending some of his followers out 2x2, as Jesus did with his followers in the Gospels. The movement grew pretty quickly, with about two thousand attending a 1910 conference.

As the movement increased, Irvine created a dual-level structure in which most members held full-time jobs and supported others designated as "workers," those who devoted themselves fully to 2x2 missionary endeavors. Edward Cooney, who was one of the early leaders of the group, disagreed with this change and split off. He, too, however, refused to name his group, which outsiders generally call the Cooneyites, a designation that vividly highlights the downside of letting others come up with your label. Within just a few years, both men were kicked out of the very groups they founded. Irvine was excommunicated from the 2x2s in 1918 after he moved to Jerusalem to await Jesus' return. The ax fell on Cooney in 1928, apparently because he attempted to introduce a healing ministry to the movement, leaving the Cooneyites without a Cooney.

The 2x2s and Cooneyites are still around today, with perhaps 100,000 members worldwide (they also have no membership rolls), about half of these in North America. They meet in homes for Sunday worship, adhere to very strict lifestyle rules, believe that no salvation is available outside their group and gather for annual conventions each year, usually held in rural areas.

Members of the "No-Name Church" are pacifists. However, members of religious groups cannot gain conscientious-objector status unless they file with a government, and you can't file unless your group has a name. One irony, then, is that the "No-Name Church," which believes it is un-Christian to name their church, had to come up with a name to avoid military service, which they also believe to be un-Christian. Thus, their conscientious-objector name in the U.S. is the "Christian Conventions." In England, they have filed under the name "The Testimony of Jesus."

DID YOU KNOW?

Two Firsts for American Christianity

Lemuel Hayes was licensed as a Congregational preacher in 1780, the first African American to be certified in the United States. He pastored an all-white church, also a first in U.S. history.

AMAZING AGNES

You may not know Agnes Gonxha Bojaxhiu, but you should. Her story is an amazing tale of spreading God's love to the poorest throughout the world.

Agnes was born into a middle-class family, but the family fell into difficult financial times with her father's murder when Agnes was eight. However, her mother gave her a deep religious devotion that gave rise to an early fascination with the work of missionaries. This desire intensified throughout her teenage years, and at eighteen she joined the Sisters of Loreto, an Irish religious order, to become a missionary nun.

The following year, Agnes's dream of becoming a missionary was realized when she was sent overseas to teach geography and catechism at a missionary school. She remained there for seventeen years, including four years as the school's principal. However, she felt a strong call to extend her work to the very poor, so she left the Sisters of Loreto to fulfill this vision. Drawing on her experience in education, Agnes started a school in a deeply impoverished urban area and learned some fundamental medical skills that allowed her to bring basic health care to those too poor to afford it through the usual channels.

Agnes was soon joined in her work by some former students from the missionary school. Over the next several decades, her small band of workers multiplied into an organization numbering in the thousands. They built orphanages and schools for poor children around the world. They opened homes for lepers, the homeless, prostitutes, battered women and drug addicts in several countries. Agnes's group of Christian workers started what many believe to be the first AIDS hospice in New York City, and added hospice services for those suffering from this condition in several other cities later. Agnes even negotiated a temporary cease-fire between the Israeli army and Palestinian fighters to rescue thirty-seven children in a hospital between the battle lines. When she died a few years ago, Agnes's organization had more than 600 missions in over 120 countries.

When someone like Agnes begins with meager resources and a big vision, and builds from this to found an organization that provides services to the world's poorest in the name of Jesus, people really should know about it. But most of you probably don't know Agnes. At least, you probably don't know her by that name. She is much more recognizable by another name, one she took on when she joined the Sisters of Loreto as a teenager—Teresa. Teresa was later called Mother Teresa by her young students in the slum school she started in Calcutta, and the name stuck.

Because Mother Teresa's name is so strongly linked to her work with the dying at the Pure Heart Home for Dying Destitutes in Calcutta, India, you may not have figured out her identity from the description above. As noteworthy as her work with the dying was, it was only the tip of the iceberg. On every continent, Mother Teresa's organization, the Sisters of Charity, was, and still is, on the front line of care for the poorest of the poor.

During her life, Mother Teresa was awarded the Nobel Peace Prize, the Medal of Freedom (the highest award the U.S. grants to civilians), honorary U.S. citizenship, the Bharat Ratna (India's highest civilian award), the Templeton Prize, the Pope John XXIII Peace Prize, the Albert Schweitzer International Prize, the Congressional Gold Medal and honorary degrees from countless universities. However, the greatest earthly honor she received was when tens of thousands of Calcutta's citizens, overwhelmingly Hindu, lined the streets for a funeral procession that took her body to a simple concrete tomb inscribed with Jesus' words, "Love one another as I have loved you." The amazing work of the Sisters of Charity continues.

MARTY AND KATIE

As the old saying goes, "Behind every successful man is an ex-nun smuggled out of the convent in an empty herring barrel." At least I think that is how it goes. Some version of this story provides the beginning of the marriage between Marty and Katie, otherwise known as Martin Luther and Katharina von Bora.

☞ THE GREAT HERRING BARREL ESCAPE

The year was 1523. Several nuns at Nimbschen had heard the Reformation teaching of Luther, were convinced by it and sought to leave their convent. However, they were not permitted to leave the cloister. When Luther heard of their desire, he enlisted the help of Leonhard Koppe, a city councilor who also delivered herring to the convent. The legend is that when Herr Koppe left the convent after his delivery the night before Easter, he smuggled out twelve nuns in empty herring barrels. There were in fact twelve nuns spirited from the cloister that night, an act that was a crime punishable by death. Some versions of the tale say, however, that the runaway nuns were hidden *among* the barrels rather than *in* them. It isn't quite as cool of a story that way, so let's just say they were in the barrels.

The question that now confronted Luther was what he should do with twelve escapee-nuns, most of whom had been in a convent since a very early age. A few returned to their families. The remaining women were lodged at the home of Lucas Cranach until they could air out from confinement inside the fish barrels and until employment or husbands could be found for them. In two years, arrangements had been made for all except one—Katharina von Bora.

KATHARINA

Katharina was born of nobility, the kind that had spiffy titles but no money. She was sent to the convent at age five after her mother's death and took vows at the age of sixteen. Finding a husband for her proved to be difficult. Katharina had taken a liking to Jerome Baumgarten, but his family had serious reservations about their son marrying a former nun and he dropped out of the picture. Other suitors presented did not thrill her, so she took the initiative, telling Luther's co-reformer, Nicholas von Armsdorf, that she would be willing to marry either him or Dr. Martinus (i.e., Luther).

Neither Armsdorf nor Luther had any intentions of marriage, but Luther had been encouraging other former priests to tie the knot. It was now "put up or shut up" time for Dr. Martinus. He sought the approval of his parents, but told almost no one else about his plans. Luther and Katharina von Bora were engaged on June 13, 1525, and married the same night. Two weeks later, a public reception was held for the new bride and groom.

MARRIED LIFE AT THE BLACK CLOISTER

Dr. and Mrs. Luther took up residence in The Black Cloister, the monastery Luther had lived in while a monk, which had been presented to him as a gift. Considering that he was a forty-two-year-old former priest and she a twenty-six-year-old former nun, the two took to marriage like a German reformer to beer. At one point, Luther did allow that it was a tad disorienting after four decades of bachelorhood to wake up in the morning with a pair of pigtails on his pillow, but the marriage was a happy one. After one year, their first child was born, quickly followed by five more (two did not survive to adolescence). If you add to this a number of orphans taken into their home and numerous hosted students and others who traveled to meet the reformer, the Luther household was one busy place.

As a professor, preacher and leader of a reformation, Luther was a busy guy, and he had an annoying habit of giving away all his money to people in need. Katie (as Luther called her) took over management of the household, put her husband on a budget, and supplemented the family income by breeding cattle and operating the brewery that remained from the monastery days. She rose at 4:00 a.m. each day to get an early start on household duties, earning her the nickname "the morning star of Wittenberg." Through her skill and hard work, the family was able to stay afloat. Luther acknowledged his wife's management role by stating, "On domestic matters I defer to Katie. Otherwise, I am led by the Holy Ghost."

KATIE'S LATER YEARS

After twenty years of marriage, Luther died (1546), leaving Katie to care for the family without his salary. The request that she move out of The Black Cloister to smaller quarters was firmly rejected by Katie, but she was soon forced to flee anyway when the Schmalkaldic War began a few months after Luther's death. When she returned, the buildings had all been burned and the animals were gone.

In financial ruin, Katie borrowed money to rebuild and took in students as boarders to help pay the bills. In 1552 she was again forced to leave Wittenberg, this time because of a plague. As she neared the city of Torgau, the horses pulling her cart were spooked and she was severely injured in the fall. Mrs. Luther never fully recovered from this incident and died three years later at the age of fifty-three. Their three surviving sons became a lawyer, a theologian and a physician. The daughter, Margarethe, married a wealthy Prussian nobleman.

"I'M GONNA YODEL MY WAY TO HEAVEN"

Folks from Dr. Steve's generation can remember when anything that sounded remotely like folk or rock music in the church was enough to induce coronary failure in a significant portion of the congregation. However, no sooner had guitars and drums made their way into many sanctuaries than the floodgates opened completely. Now, without too much trouble, you can find Christian versions of rap, Goth, thrash metal and disco. Larry the Cucumber even plays the tuba for the VeggieTales theme song. This led us to wonder whether any style from the vast musical universe had escaped takeover by Christian musicians. Below are the partial results of our exhaustive investigations.

Perhaps the most remarkable act of Christian musical redemption has been the panpipes. Throughout history, the panpipes have had a satanic connotation. The pagan god Pan, with his horns and cloven hooves, was often representative of the devil. And he is always pictured playing the panpipes (Pan/panpipes—get it?) to entice the unsuspecting to do his evil bidding. Today, however, many have questioned why the devil should have all the good panpipe music. So if you have a hankering for some mellow, easy-listening panpipe arrangements of Christian music to meditate by, it's out there.

The legendary country-swing master, Bob Wills, titled one of his songs, "Will There Be Yodeling in Heaven?" While there is no definitive answer to this question yet, you can buy a CD with a song titled, "I'm Gonna Yodel My Way to Heaven," performed by Yodeling Theresa. So if Sister Theresa is right, we can at least get our yodeling fix in transit to the pearly gates. If you like a more sophisticated form of yodeling, you can catch Larry the Cucumber singing "The Yodeling Veterinarian of the Alps" on one of the VeggieTales videos. It turns out that Larry is a lot more musically versatile than anyone suspected.

Into reggae, Mon? The steel drums are now playing for Jah (God), and Christian reggae is one of the fastest growing segments of that market. While many still associate this musical genre with those bizarre dreadlocks and the Rastafarians with their belief that Haile Selassie is an incarnation of God (not to mention a close connection with ganja), reggae's roots are definitely in gospel. And reggae's return to its roots is more evident all the time. The great

Bob Marley hooked up with the Ethiopian Orthodox Church toward the end of his life, and some of the hottest reggae artists of the day, such as Christafari (who played at the 1997 presidential inauguration) and Lt. Stitchie, offer a clear Christian message in their music. Christian reggae? Jah, Mon. Nothing to dread here.

Anyone who thinks that a Catholic Mass would be too formal and stuffy for them hasn't experienced the Polka Mass, which has been performed all over the world, including at St. Peter's Basilica in Rome. Forget Carnegie Hall. When you play the Vatican, you've made it musically. If you missed the Polka Mass when it came to your town, you can still get recordings of the music performed by the Polka Masters and sung by the Perkatones. It's the ultimate in mass appeal, so "Roll out the Bible."

This list may lead you to believe that no musical style has been untouched by Christian hands, but we did find an opening for musicians willing to blast into new frontiers. So far, we have not been able to find a Christian ukulele artist. If you are interested in filling this conspicuous gap, the road has been paved for you already. Simply order "Jumpin' Jim's Ukulele Spirit" and take advantage of ukulele arrangements for forty hymns, spirituals and songs of inspiration, and you are on your way.

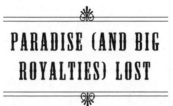

PARADISE (AND BIG ROYALTIES) LOST

Do you wish you had listened to your brother-in-law's advise about investing in Microsoft's IPO back in 1986 (you would now have about three hundred shares for each share you bought at twenty-one dollars)? Did you miss the last real-estate boom? Don't feel too bad; even really bright people blow some great financial opportunities, even when they are right in front of them. Case in point: John Milton.

No one is quite sure when blind poet John Milton penned *Paradise Lost*, but it was probably somewhere between 1650 and 1660. It wasn't until 1667, however, when the epic poem, which recounts Satan's rebellion against God and the fall of humanity, was first published. A printer, Samuel Simmons, agreed to pay Milton five pounds for the rights to publish the work and an additional five pounds for each impression. At this time, the British government limited printings to 1,500 per impression, but even with these restrictions, the first edition seemed destined to be the last as well because of slow sales.

The sluggish sales of *Paradise Lost*'s first edition can be chalked up to several factors. First, Milton was a participant in the Puritan rebellion against Charles I and, in fact, did some prison time for his antiroyalist views. A lot of potential buyers weren't quite ready to forgive and forget. Second, because of the length of the poem, Milton wrote in blank verse rather than in a more conventional poetic style, which was a bit off-putting to potential read-ers. Finally, the first edition had no critical apparatus to help read-ers navigate the long and difficult text.

The second edition, which came out in 1674, mitigated some of the problems of the first by including annotations, adding a plot introduction for each book, and dividing books VII and X into two, bringing the total to twelve books. This was the last edition to appear during Milton's life; he died later in 1674, bringing his total take for *Paradise Lost* to ten pounds.

☛ PARADISE POST-MILTON

Simmons produced two more editions of *Paradise Lost* in the next five years, for which Milton's widow received ten pounds. She then agreed to sell him the copyright for eight pounds. Sim-mons, who thought that sales of *Paradise Lost* had peaked out,

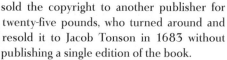

sold the copyright to another publisher for twenty-five pounds, who turned around and resold it to Jacob Tonson in 1683 without publishing a single edition of the book.

Most believe that Tonson purchased the copyright to the book more for his apprecia-tion of Milton's artistry than for hopes of turn-ing it into a bestseller. However, he took sev-eral steps to make *Paradise Lost* more accessible to a general audience, including in-dexes and an explanatory introduction, and sales soon went through the roof. Tonson put out a wide variety of editions, including several illustrated versions of *Paradise Lost*, and made a considerable for-tune on the poem that earned the author only ten pounds.

All good things must come to an end, however. In 1709, Parlia-ment passed a law that limited the copyrights for works from deceased authors to twenty-one years. The Tonson family waged a running battle against the law and managed to keep editions of *Paradise Lost* from other publishers off the market for the next forty years. These efforts finally failed in 1749, and within a decade the Tonson-family publishing house went broke and closed down. This was obviously not the end for *Paradise Lost*. It is generally thought to be the most widely read epic poem produced in the English language. You can read it online—if you purchase Microsoft Word.

A LITTLE PAPAL TRIVIA

Nations and empires come and go, and we consider it a marvel when a social or political structure endures for several centuries. In this context, the longevity of the papacy is a pretty amazing thing, even for Christians who do not trace the office back to the apostle Peter.

By official Roman Catholic reckoning, there have been 267 popes (265 different individuals—see below about one who became pope three different times) stretching back over a period of almost two thousand years. Coming up with an official number is tricky because of the lack of record keeping in the church's early years, not to mention several points at which it was not really clear which pope was actually pope. When you consider a span of this length with the number of individuals holding this office, some interesting bits of trivia are bound to arise.

☛ WHAT HAPPENED TO XX?

One of the best-loved and most influential popes in recent decades was Pope John XXIII (d. 1963). However, he was actually only the twenty-second pontiff to assume the name John. There was no Pope John XX. The most commonly accepted theory about why XX was skipped is that two different dates had been assigned to an earlier Pope John, leading historians in the eleventh century to believe that this referred to two different individuals. Thus, when Peter of Spain (ironically from Portugal, the only Portuguese pope in history) took the name John XXI, the number became so closely associated with his reign that it created less confusion to skip over John XX than to renumber the succession of Johns.

As it was, John XXI was only pope for nine months. He was in his library alone one evening when the ceiling collapsed on him, injuring him so severely that he died six days later in the year 1277. By the way, even if you make the adjustment for the missing John XX, John is still the most common papal name, followed by Gregory and Benedict in a tie for second place (we've had sixteen of each).

☛ QUICK SUCCESSION

While Pope John XXI's nine months is briefer than most, it is not the shortest pontifical tenure. Many may remember from recent history that John Paul I (d. 1978) died only thirty-three days after becoming pope. However, the winner of the shortest papal reign contest is Stephen II (d. 752), who died somewhere between one to four days (reports conflict) after ascending to the office. Some have stayed around a bit longer. Pius IX was pope from 1846 to 1878, thirty-two years.

The youngest pope was Benedict IX, the nephew of two previous popes. Roman Catholic sources place his age at around eighteen, but many sources say that his actual age was either eleven or twelve at his ascent to the papacy. Benedict IX also has the dubious distinction of being pope three different times. He became pope in 1032, but abdicated his role in 1044, quite possibly to marry. He quickly decided that he had made a bad move, forced his successor out of Rome the next year and retook the throne. In more political intrigue, he later was deposed, and later regained the papacy.

There is some argument about which pope was the oldest, but many put the age of Celestine III at eighty-five when he took office. He lived another seven years. Of the 265 individuals who have been pope, 205 have been Italian or Roman, including every pontiff from 1431 to 1978, as far as can be ascertained. The French are well behind in second place, with nineteen popes.

☞ HOW ARE POPES ELECTED?

The current method of electing popes goes back to the thirteenth century, when they were having a difficult time agreeing on a pontiff. In fact, on one occasion it took about eighteen months to come to an agreement, and this occurred only after the cardinals were locked into a room and refused exit until they finished their appointed task. In fact, the word *conclave,* used to describe the selection process, is derived from the Latin for "locked room."

In recent centuries, conclaves are called no later than eighteen days following the death of a pope. This meeting takes place in the famed Sistine Chapel, and no one is allowed in or out during the deliberations. The decision is made by 120 cardinals, who are assisted in their discussions by a few attendants. No one present is allowed to reveal anything about the discussions. The voting is secret and requires a majority of two-thirds plus one. If a vote does not yield the necessary majority, the paper ballots are burned with wet paper and wood chips, which creates the black smoke that signals to the outside world that everyone will be in the Sistine Chapel for a bit longer. When a single candidate receives the requisite number of votes, only the ballots are burned, which produces the famous white smoke announcing the election of a pope. The new pope assumes his responsibilities immediately.

☞ WHO IS THE POPE HERE?

There have been several times throughout the history of the Roman Catholic Church when multiple individuals simultaneously have claimed to be pope. However, none of these situations was as serious as what is often called the "Great Schism." In the fourteenth century, the papacy was relocated from Rome to Avignon, France, and remained there for about a seventy-year period under the tight control of the French monarchy. This was a festering insult to the Italians until Pope Gregory XI moved the papacy back to Rome in 1377. However, he died the next year, and the citizens of Rome were concerned (with justification) that the French cardinals would attempt to orchestrate a move back to Avignon. Fearing that a riot would break out unless an Italian was elected, the cardinals elevated an Italian as pope. However, later that same year, the same group of cardinals, most of whom were French, elected a rival pope who promptly moved back to Avignon.

For the next thirty-one years, competing papacies existed in Avignon and Rome, which obviously created tremendous confusion. The situation became so intolerable that a council met at Pisa in 1409 to straighten everything out. They deposed the rival popes at Avignon and Rome, and elected a new pope. The only glitch in this plan was that no one really figured out how to get the other two popes to actually step down. As a result, there were three claimants to the papacy for the next eight years—one in Rome, one in Avignon and one in Pisa. Finally, the Council of Constance deposed the popes in France and Pisa and pressured the Roman pope to resign, clearing the path for the reunification of the papacy in Rome in 1417.

☞ MARRIED POPES?

Catholicism's requirement that clergy, the pope included, live a life of celibacy is well known. Not a lot of people realize that there was no official mandate for celibacy until several centuries after the birth of the church, even though the tradition of celibacy was strongly established much earlier. In light of this, it is interesting that Peter, claimed by Catholicism as the first pope, was married (1 Corinthians 9:5; Mark 1:30). It is even acknowledged in Catholicism that some of the early popes who followed Peter were married; some sources claim up to forty married popes.

It is impossible to come up with an accurate count of married popes because of lack of clear information about many early pontiffs and the possibility that historical sources were suppressed after the marriage ban became official. However, it was not until Pope Gregory VII in the eleventh century that clerical celibacy was required, and this edict was codified by the Second Lateran Council in 1139.

Also, while it does not apply directly to the question of the papacy, since 1980, married Protestant pastors who convert to Catholicism can be ordained as priests without giving up their marriage and children. Several have taken this step, and there are indeed married Roman Catholic priests throughout the world. None of these married priests, however, are considered strong candidates to become the next pontiff.

GOD ON THE AIR

Radio station KDKA began broadcasts on November 2, 1920, from its studio, which was actually a small shack constructed on a Westinghouse factory roof in Pittsburgh, Pennsylvania. Exactly two months later, on January 2, 1921, the first religious service in history was transmitted over its radio frequency.

One of the engineers at Westinghouse was a member of Calvary Episcopal Church in Pittsburgh, and arranged to have their Sunday evening vespers service broadcast. The senior pastor, Edwin Van Ettin, wasn't too keen on the idea, so his associate, Lewis B. Whittemore, led the service that evening. Two technicians sent from KDKA to assist with the program, a Jew and a Catholic, were dressed in choir robes to make them less conspicuous. This first venture in religious broadcasting went over so well that Calvary Episcopal's vespers service became a regular Sunday night feature on KDKA, and continued for forty-one years. It didn't take long for Reverend Van Ettin to be sold on it, either. Once he saw how popular it was, he nudged his associate aside and became the regular preacher for the service.

MOVE OVER ESPN

KDKA had a number of "firsts" in radio history. It was the first to air a presidential inaugural address (Warren G. Harding) and a sporting event, a ten-round boxing match between Johnny Ray and Johnny Dundee. However, the broadcast of Calvary Episcopal's service came two months prior to the inaugural address, and three months before the first public broadcast of a sporting event. In fact, religion on the radio even predates what Dr. Steve considers the other form of religious broadcasting, professional baseball on the radio, by about eight months. KDKA was also the first to do *that,* airing play-by-play from Forbes field between the Philadelphia Phillies and the Pittsburgh Pirates. Pittsburgh won eight to five. Thus, one might say that when it comes to radio history, preachers preceded presidents, pugilists and Pirates' play-by-play. Just make sure no one is standing in front of you when you say it, though.

In radio's early days, many preachers were reluctant to take to the airwaves, and more than a few considered it to be the voice of Satan. It seems clear that Christianity has overcome whatever radio-phobia it might have had in the past. Today, almost two thousand radio stations (of a total of around fourteen thousand) are categorized by Arbitron as religious stations. And hold on to your hat, Garth Brooks. Christian radio is right behind country music stations in number, and closing fast.

DID YOU KNOW?

How Not to De-program a Dominican

Perhaps the most famous member of the Dominican order is Thomas Aquinas, who had to overcome significant family resistance to join. The Dominicans took their poverty pretty seriously, and Aquinas's very wealthy family didn't think it would reflect well on the family if he entered the order. Thomas's brothers, both soldiers, kidnapped him and took him to a family castle where they spent the better part of two years trying to dissuade him from becoming a Dominican. At one point, they hired a prostitute to seduce him and divert him from his vows. Aquinas, as the story goes, chased her out of his cell with a hot poker taken from the fireplace. His family finally relented. Aquinas joined the Dominicans and was eventually proclaimed the authoritative philosopher of the Roman Catholic Church.

LOTS OF WIVES, A BUNCH OF EXECUTIONS AND A BOOK (EPISODE II)

In our last episode (see p. 39), Henry VIII had died and left his ten-year-old son, Edward VI, as king. Henry had made the English church independent of Rome, so when Sir Thomas More and Bishop John Fisher argued that the church should return to the jurisdiction of Rome, Henry had them beheaded. At the same time, Henry did not want England's church to become Protestant, so when Robert Barnes and John Frith urged Henry to move in that direction, Henry carefully considered their case, and had them beheaded also. Cranmer, who had argued for leniency for both sides, was caught in the middle of this mess.

☞ THE MOVE TOWARD PROTESTANTISM

Edward VI, it turned out, had absorbed his mother's Protestant sympathies, and the king's advisors encouraged Cranmer to cautiously move the English church in that direction. The main innovation came in 1549 when the *Book of Common Prayer*, prepared largely through the efforts of Cranmer, was introduced. The *Book of Common Prayer* (or more precisely, *The Book of Common Prayer, and the Administration of Sacraments, and Other Rites and Ceremonies of the Church*) was so named because (1) it was in English, the common language of the nation, thus replacing Latin services, and (2) it was to be the only book used in all English churches, which previously had allowed use of various prayer books. A second edition was introduced in 1552 and was even more pronounced in its Protestant sympathies. This edition is essentially the same *Book of Common Prayer* used worldwide today in Anglican/Episcopalian churches.

Up to this point, British politics (both ecclesiastical and secular) had been a contact sport, but things were considerably calmer during Edward VI's reign. The push and pull between Catholicism and Protestantism was still present, but Edward was much less inclined than his father to lop off the craniums of those who disagreed with him, much to Cranmer's relief. Cranmer's wife was also allowed to come back home.

The brief respite from executions and banishments came to an abrupt end with Edward's death in 1553 at the age of sixteen. With no male in the line of succession, Cranmer supported Lady Jane Grey as queen. However, she was overthrown after only nine days and replaced by Edward's half-sister Mary, a.k.a. "Bloody Mary" (who should not be confused with the drink by the same name made from tomato juice and vodka).

As you may recall from episode one, Mary was the daughter of Catherine of Aragon, Henry's first wife. Because of the divorce, Catherine had been sent away in disgrace and Mary had lost her legitimacy, and she was pretty sore at Cranmer about all this. In addition, she was very Catholic and not at all amused by Cranmer's *Book of Common Prayer*. This was definitely not good news for the archbishop. It wasn't very good news for Mary's "Nine-Day Queen" predecessor either. Mary had Lady Jane beheaded and buried between the two headless former queens we met in episode one, Anne Boleyn and Catherine Howard.

☛ CRANMER CHANGES HIS MIND, AND THEN CHANGES HIS MIND AGAIN

Mary immediately set out to reverse all the Protestant innovations, reinstating the Latin Mass and banning the *Book of Common Prayer.* When Cranmer objected, Mary was presented with the opportunity to do what she had been itching to do for years. She had Cranmer arrested and thrown in jail, where he languished for two years. Under intense pressure, which included getting a roof-side seat to see two of his buddies burned at the stake, Cranmer was eventually persuaded to sign six recantations, each progressively putting more distance between himself and Protestantism. Cranmer was promised his freedom for signing the recantations, but Bloody Mary was not exactly the forgiving kind. She reneged on her agreement and condemned Cranmer to be burned at the stake despite his recantations.

As you might guess, the burning of a former archbishop of Canterbury was a significant public event, and Mary, hoping to maximize Cranmer's humiliation, allowed him to preach to the assembled throng and announce his renunciation of Protestantism. This was a big miscalculation on Mary's part, because Cranmer instead used the opportunity to recant his recantations and reaffirmed his Protestant leanings. When finally chained to the stake, Cranmer thrust his right hand down into the growing flames, stating that the hand that had performed the offensive deed of signing the recantations should burn first. It did, if you don't count his feet and legs.

With Cranmer burned at the stake (one of three hundred to die in this manner during Mary's bloody reign) and a Catholic queen firmly in place, it looked like the end for Protestantism in England. However, Mary died childless after a five-year reign and her half-sister Elizabeth (daughter of the now-headless Anne Boleyn) ascended to the throne. Queen Elizabeth I (not the ocean liner) brought the English church back into the Protestant fold and reinstated use of the *Book of Common Prayer.*

☞ THE *BOOK OF COMMON PRAYER*

As Anglicanism became established in England and spread into North America and Africa through colonial activities, Cranmer's enduring contribution, the *Book of Common Prayer*, played a central role in holding this communion together. In addition to liturgies for various types of services within the church (such as baptism, the Eucharist and ordinations), the *Book of Common Prayer* includes the Psalms in their entirety and pivotal New Testament texts, a lectionary that provides daily Scripture readings that cover the entire Bible every two years, and the 39 Articles of Religion, outlining the doctrinal views of the Anglican/Episcopal Church.

There are currently seventy million Anglicans/Episcopalians in over 150 countries, each using the prayer book. More copies of the *Book of Common Prayer* may exist in the English language than any book except the Bible (although we do not concern ourselves with such trivial matters in this book). It also has been translated into dozens of other languages, including Swahili, Mohawk, Kashmiri, Telugu and Esperanto. Cranmer was burned at the stake in large part because of the *Book of Common Prayer*, but his legacy lives on through it.

DID YOU KNOW?
America's First Saint

Mother Frances Xavier Cabrini was the first U.S. citizen to be canonized as a saint by the Roman Catholic Church. She was born in Italy, the youngest of fifteen children. Mother Frances, who came to the U.S. at about forty years of age to work with the large numbers of Italians immigrating to this country, founded numerous hospitals, schools and orphanages. Like so many of these immigrants, she took on U.S. citizenship (1909). She was canonized in 1946.

SALVATION MOUNTAIN

One immutable truth of the universe is that Christians on a mission ask for donations. But what do you make of someone who asks for donations in the form of paint (preferably acrylic, in bright colors)? Obviously, you will probably conclude that this is a rather unique mission, and it is. You see, Leonard Knight has built a mountain, a salvation mountain to be precise, and he needs to keep it painted. If this doesn't make much sense yet, maybe we should start from the beginning.

☞ THE ODD ODYSSEY OF LEONARD KNIGHT

Leonard Knight was a restless Vermonter who had bounced around in jobs following a stint in the Korean War. In 1967, Jesus caught up with Leonard while Leonard was visiting his sister in San Diego. A couple of years later, a hot-air balloon sailing overhead gave Leonard an idea of how he could tell people about Jesus' love. For almost twenty years, the idea stuck in his mind, and he eventually had a massive balloon built with the words "God is Love" emblazoned on it. Then, in 1986, he headed for the Mojave Desert east of San Diego to launch it so that people from miles around could see the message. One minor problem: there just aren't many people in the Mojave to look at a balloon. Another minor problem: even if anyone would have been close enough to see it, the huge balloon was too heavy to get off the ground.

Knight's Plan B was to hang around another week—just long

enough to construct an eight-foot tall monument. But it just kept growing. His first attempt, a concrete mound, collapsed from the weight. Undeterred, he started over using adobe constructed from clay and straw, and "Salvation Mountain" grew up to be about forty feet high and one hundred feet wide.

At the top of Salvation Mountain is a large cross. Front and center below the cross is the balloon's original message—"God is love"—and immediately under that is a large heart with the prayer, "Jesus I'm a sinner. Please come upon my body and into my heart." On the sides are slogans and lots of painted flowers and trees, with waterfalls cascading down on one side into "the ocean blue." Steps are built into the side to make it one very large interactive and extremely colorful work of art.

☞ TWENTY YEARS LATER

As for the mountain, Leonard is pretty much done with the construction phase. He has plenty of other things to do, like painting and more painting. It's not just his mountain that needs constant repainting (the paint soaks in); his old dump truck—on the back of which is Leonard's house (with no electricity)—and his jeep are also colorful collages of Bible quotes and words like *Bible, love* and *Jesus.* Knight estimates that he has put about 100,000 gallons of paint on Salvation Mountain and his vehicles.

If you are thinking that 100,000 gallons of paint is quite at bit, you are not alone. In the early 1990s, Imperial County officials, noting that Knight just happened to be a squatter on government property, wanted the site declared a toxic hazard site because of all the paint. The plan was to bulldoze Salvation Mountain in California's Mojave Desert and haul it off to a toxic burial site in Nevada's Mojave Desert. Public outcry soon put an end to that proposal. In fact, the fate of Salvation Mountain took a dramatic turn, and has now been entered into the Congressional Record as a national treasure. Now would be an appropriate time to shake your head and say, "Only in America."

Knight is still out there in the Mojave, painting his mountain and warmly welcoming guests who come to see its colorful proclamation of God's love. Now in his midseventies, he plans to be out there until he dies. So if you've got an extra gallon of acrylic in Ocean Blue from your last home-improvement project, Leonard's accepting donations. He knows just the place for it.

Now if we could just get them to take donations of Windex at the Crystal Cathedral . . .

WHEN IS EASTER?

Most of us like it when the dates of holidays stay put, like Christmas, New Year's Day and Valentine's Day. Most of us eventually get it straight that Thanksgiving is the third Thursday of November, but it gets trickier with holidays like Labor Day that have now been attached to Mondays so we can snag a three-day weekend.

The holiday that leaves most people scratching their heads, however, is Easter. The date of this holiday changes every year and can even fall in two different months. This gets even more confusing in more liturgical churches since the dates of other holidays (Ascension Sunday, Pentecost, etc.) are calculated in reference to the date of Easter. So how is the date of Easter Sunday determined?

Here is the formula: Easter Sunday is the first Sunday that follows a full moon that occurs on or after the vernal equinox, which is March 21. The first full moon that comes on or after the vernal equinox can transpire anytime from March 21 through April 18, which means that Easter Sunday can fall anytime on or between March 22 and April 25. Simple enough, right?

☞ JUST TO COMPLICATE MATTERS

The formula above is based on what is called the ecclesiastical full moon, since it is possible for the astronomical full moon to fall on two different dates in different places around the world. Also, this method of calculating Easter relies on the Gregorian calendar, which was not widely accepted until 1583, so it only gets you to the dates of Easter for about four hundred years in the past. Before this time, the date when Easter was celebrated varied by region. Moreover, the Orthodox Church still uses the Julian calendar. Thus, sometimes Easter is celebrated in Orthodox churches on the same date as in the Western church, but it can also occur up to five weeks later!

☞ WORK IT OUT YOURSELF

Now if you want to complicate matters a bit more and find out when Easter Sunday will occur in the future in the Western church, the following algorithm (published anonymously in the journal *Nature*, in 1876) allows you to work it out, provided you have a calculator and a bit of time. Once you get it figured out for the next 5,700,000 years, you can relax because the cycle then repeats.

a = year%19
b = year/100
c = year%100
d = b/4
e = b%4
f = (b+8)/25
g = (b-f+1)/3
h = (19*a+b-d-g+15)%30
i = c/4
k = c%4
l = (32+2*e+2*i-h-k)%7
m = (a+11*h+22*l)/451
Easter Month = (h+l-7*m+114)/31 [3 = March, 4 = April]
p = (h+l-7*m+114)%31
Easter Date = p+1   (date in Easter Month)

(The symbol / represents an integer division neglecting the remainder, while % is division keeping only the remainder. So 30/7 = 4, and 30%7 = 2. Got that?)

☞ EASTER FOR DUMMIES

For most of us, the best bet is just to buy a calendar that has Easter Sunday clearly marked. If you go to the store and see chocolate bunnies on sale for half price, you've probably missed it. The upshot of all this is that if the date of Valentine's Day was as complicated as Easter, every male in the world would be in big trouble.

ANSWERS

KEY FOR "MOTTOS"

1. Azusa Pacific University—(c) "God First, Since 1899." This makes it sound like God finally pulled into the lead a little over a century ago after lagging for a while. The school seems to have suppressed any information about who or what was first prior to 1899. Actually, the real motto is simply "God First," but it often appears around the campus with the founding date closely attached, creating a bit of confusion.

2. United Church of Christ—(e) "That they may all be one." This is the UCC's traditional motto. Recently, however, they have been using the motto "Never put a period where God has put a comma." Notice that since this statement is from that renowned theologian Gracie Allen, and not God, it ends with a period, which comes right after "comma."

3. Salvation Army—(f) "Blood and Fire." This historical motto refers to the saving blood of Jesus, and fire, which represents the Holy Spirit's help in living holy lives. Apparently "blood and fire" hasn't been playing well in focus groups recently because the Salvation Army is now using "Heart to God, Hand to Man" as a motto.

4. Christian Church (Disciples of Christ)—(b) "Where the Scriptures speak, we speak; where the Scriptures are silent, we are silent." The silence of Scripture on many matters explains why you can't get an answer from members of this denomination about how to get to Sixth and Main.

5. University of Notre Dame—(i) *Crux spes unica* (The cross is the only hope). This comes from a university whose football team gave a whole new meaning to "Hail Mary."

6. United Methodist Church—(g) "Open Hearts. Open Minds. Open Doors." This is also the mission statement for a hotel doorman in

New York City who moonlights as a cardiologist and psychologist.

7. American Council of Christian Churches—(a) "Earnestly Contending for the Faith." This ecumenical group's constitution excludes from membership any denomination that is included in the National Council of Churches, World Council of Churches or the World Evangelical Fellowship, as well as any congregation from "the modern Charismatic Movement or the Ecumenical Movement." When an ecumenical group cuts out anyone from the "Ecumenical Movement," it seems to indicate that the motto "Earnestly Contentious about the Faith" might be a tad more accurate.

8. Baylor University—(h) *Pro Ecclesia, Pro Texana* (For Church, For Texas). Bet you didn't know there was a Latin word for Texas. Of course, anyone knows that Texas comes in a close second to the church. Rumor is that some Texans are trying to change the motto because it just seems too redundant. Trinity College broadens the motto a bit with *Pro Ecclesia et Patria* (For Church and Country).

9. Holt International—(j) "Every child deserves a home." Consider this a public service announcement. If you have ever thought about adoption, Holt is a terrific Christian organization placing children from across the globe with caring families. They gave Dr. Steve and his wife the two greatest children in the world, but I'm sure they have plenty of good ones left for you.

10. Campus Crusade for Christ—(d) "Win the Campus for Christ Today, Win the World for Christ Tomorrow." This explains why Campus Crusade folks are never quite sure what to do on Wednesdays.

KEY TO "FAMILIAR PHRASES"

1. Isaiah 40:15

2. Nope. The phrase is old and the origin unknown.

3. It's in there. Even though it sounds like a reference to actors' dialogue lines for *Baywatch*, it is found in Psalm 8:2.

4. This is not from Eve in the Garden of Eden, or anywhere else in Scripture.

5. Origin: Probably a Cubs fan.

6. This is Aristotle, and "swallow" here refers to a type of bird.

7. Ecclesiastes 10:1

8. That's Patrick Henry. Apparently, old Pat got this liberty/death thing confused as a multiple-choice question. In reality, he got both because he lived to see the U.S. become a free country and then died in 1799.

9. Jeremiah 31:29

10. Job 19:20. Bet you didn't know the Bible was so interested in teeth.

11. Thankfully this is not the Bible, but the philosopher Sartre. The sentiment is widely shared, however, by anyone currently living in a dorm situation.

12. A lot of people are surprised, but it's not in the Bible.

13. Matthew 15:14

14. The Bible never refers to cats, which is one critical sign of its divine inspiration.

15. Shakespeare, *Hamlet* (5.1). However, while cats are shut out of Scripture, dogs do make the Bible, mostly returning to their own vomit. See Proverbs 26:11 and 2 Peter 2:22.

16. Ezekiel 18:2

17. No, but it has religious origins. In Jewish and Islamic traditions, the seventh heaven is the highest level of that celestial realm.

18. You have five choices here: Exodus 4:15; Deuteronomy 18:18; 2 Samuel 14:3, 19; and Jeremiah 1:9.

19. Numbers 22:31

20. That would be Yogi Berra, whose quotes have biblical status in New York only.

Scoring—Number Correct

16-20—Not too bad.

12-15—Maybe you ought to spend a little more time reading your Bible.

8-11—Maybe you ought to have a little visit with your pastor.

0-7—Maybe you ought to have a long visit with Billy Graham.

KEY TO "GREAT OPENING LINES"

1. g (Esther)

2. c (Ruth)

3. a (Hebrews)

4. k (Genesis)—That one should have been a "gimme."

5. l (Zephaniah)—This one should definitely not be a lectionary reading for a Monday morning.

6. f (Gospel of John)

7. e (1 Chronicles)—The opening verse is just one word too long to qualify for the shortest verse in the Bible.

8. i (2 John)

9. b (Song of Solomon)—There's an opening line that makes you want to keep reading.

10. j (Ezekiel)

11. d (Psalms)

12. h (Acts of the Apostles)

Bonus question: Galatians